Going Nomad

Because Life Can BE an Extended Vacation

Written With Love
By

SAKSHIN

Going Nomad Published by Wellness Spectrum Publishing
First Edition November 2015
Copyright © 2015 by (Wellness Spectrum Pub.)

ALL RIGHTS RESERVED. One or more global copyright treaties protect the information in this document. This book is not intended to provide exact details or advice. This report is for informational purposes only. Author reserves the right to make any changes necessary to maintain the integrity of the information held within. This Special Report is not presented as legal or accounting advice. All rights reserved, including the right of reproduction in whole or in part in any form. No parts of this book may be reproduced in any form without written permission of the copyright owner.

NOTICE OF LIABILITY

In no event shall the author or the publisher be responsible or liable for any loss of profits or other commercial or personal damages, including but not limited to special incidental, consequential, or any other damages, in connection with or arising out of furnishing, performance or use of this book.

ISBN 978-0-9934557-0-4

Printed in USA

TABLE OF CONTENTS

Foreword

Preface	1
Introduction	3
Chapter 1 HOW TO FIND WHO YOU ARE	5
Chapter 2 TRAVELING STYLES	23
Chapter 3 HOW AND WHERE TO START. HOW TO PLAN AND HAVE FUN DOING IT	39
Chapter 4 EARLING MONEY WHILE TRAVELING	59
Chapter 5 THE NEW LIFE BEGINS	71
Chapter 6 HOW TO DEAL WITH PROBLEMS ALONG THE WAY	85
Chapter 7 WHEN THE NOMAD MUST GO HOME	97
Chapter 8 THE EXPAT EXPERIENCE	109
Chapter 9 IS TIME TO LET YOU PLAY	119
Appendix	126
Photo Credits	132
Resources	134

GOING NOMAD

FOREWORD

Dear Reader,

I have known the author of this booklet, Sakshin, for many years. He never ceases to surprise me with his immense wisdom and creative endeavour. When he first told me he wanted to write a series of books on the traveler's lifestyles, I immediately recognized that it was the project of his entire lifetime. Traveling shaped him into the person he is today. I was afraid he would give out too much in his books, especially in the first one you now holding in your hands. I could not have been more mistaken; the book is crafted so to give just enough information that it can be easily digested. It is a very practical book intended for reading more than once and perhaps for carrying with you once you are indeed on your own epic travel journey!

Sakshin is a very unusual guy, at first appearing distant and aloof. While he fools people with his demeanour, he is instead a careful observer, ready to intervene when is needed with his humour, warmth, wisdom, and the most essential (even cruel at times) kick in the butt.

So don't be surprised if this attitude is translated into his prose. I enjoyed tremendously how he switches from authoritative to fatherly to insane, all within few paragraphs at times, as it makes reading this book quite unique. If there is one suggestion, I can provide to his readers, it is to pause often. Have a recording device, such as a cell phone or simply pen and paper, and once you have ideas, jot them down or record them. It is not a complicated narrative, so you can take time in your pauses and still get back reading without losing track.

I am amazed by how Sakshin condensed his work, stripping it down to the bare essentials of what it means to travel for an extended period of time. I now feel inclined to travel myself, and I am so glad I have Sakshin to coach me through the process. This book is a baby step, although a giant one, towards getting you on the road very quickly. Possibly if the author had indulged his readers by giving more thorough information, the readers would feel paralyzed and overwhelmed. Instead, once finishing *Going Nomad*, you feel refreshed, as though your journey has already begun.

Jenny, London

PREFACE

Nomadic lifestyles are no longer restricted to gypsies or indigenous tribes. If you associate the word "nomad" with romantic love stories like in *Lawrence of Arabia*, your guesses would be--for the most part--wrong. While exotic destinations are within your reach (as well as adventures and the opportunity for intense romance), for twenty-first century nomads, travel is a way of life. True nomads are horrified by five-star settings and short, luxury vacations. Instead, their way of life has a conscience, requiring immersion in foreign cultures, and a respect for nature and its preservation. You might find a nomad happily spending a few months working in a conservation reserve or learning organic and permaculture farming. Yet, don't be surprised if the same nomad owns a villa on the ocean shore.

This emerging trend of leaving urban areas to see the world has made the dream of traveling a reality for many people. The World Wide Web has enabled people to work from anywhere and retiring early is on the increase, as is going from start-up to stardom in a very short while. More and more entrepreneurs are in a position to take many months off each calendar year and become part-time nomads, although they might not necessarily recognize themselves as such.

Nomads are a new kind of traveler. I use both words (nomad and traveler), to mean very similar concepts; the main difference is, however, that travelers usually begin their journeys by bumping around aimlessly, while a true nomad moves deliberately from place to place, settling for a while to soak in the local culture, and gains new skills continuously. They often use their time in each new place to work, in very creative ways towards a fairer, better world. They leave only footprints, although their often-invisible interactions contribute somehow to co-create a sustainable, Eco-friendly future. Since both nomads and travelers on the road are at first indistinguishable, I justify the usage of both words in the book; travelers will eventually grow into nomads if their calling is true,and their intentions are genuine.

I have created this book because, although you cannot turn nomadic overnight, with very little guidance you can get on the road at lightning speed. You will soon discover many things to consider and plan before and during a trip. Whether you're planning a trip lasting three months, six months, or a year or even if you want to go nomad full-time and never go home at all—the exercises, tips, and real stories in this little book will help you. If you are a beginner, you will love the simple steps narrated in the following pages, as long as you remind yourself that implementing their wisdom will get you on the road in no time. For the more *"seasoned traveler"*, contained in this book you might find reminders of what you already know as well as new insights and perhaps even few gems of wisdom to consider and to implement into your travel.

I have experienced first-hand the truth in the popular statement *"traveling broadens your mind"*. Traveling gives you an education that is parallel to none. The coolest thing is that this knowledge and wisdom is available to anyone open enough to receive it. No matter your age or background, you will find something in each travel experience that can tremendously enrich your life.

In this book, I am going to write about how to transition from the life you work for, to the life you enjoy by opening a doorway. You are invited to crossover it to fully absorb the lessons, the teachings that traveling gives you. You will not be able to resist the temptations; you will be thirsty to see for yourself and to experience the wonders and the pitfalls I share with you in this book.

Most of us currently live their life by taking advantage of commodities and comfort. We seem to have lost touch with the fundamentals of so-called *"human nature"*: adapting and surviving within our environment. Unless we travel, we cannot broaden and develop this skill that we all inherit. Take it like upgrading the operating system to Nomad 2.0--its users will never fear any hostile environment again, instead will use the experience for their own personal growth. They will actively adapt to, interact with, and influence the foreign culture they cross paths with during their journey.

"Not all those who wander are lost",
a line from the poem "All that is gold does not glitter", as written in The Lord of the Rings by J R. R. Tolkien.

Introduction

MY name is Sakshin, a Sanskrit word meaning "to witness." I do love listening and observing, and I believe we all learn more when we remain objective and open to new experiences. Professionally, I'm a coach, a health consultant, and an advisor on spiritual development. I look for the magic in small things, try to find harmony and balance in chaos, and help others to do the same.

I was born in Italy and have had the travel bug since I was a teenager. At sixteen, I learned how five hundred dollars could finance a leisurely, month-long stay on a Greek island. I repeated the whole experience twice in the following years until I finished schooling. By then, my English was good enough to move abroad.

At eighteen, I moved to London, which I chose in part because flights originating from this city were cheap. Also, the job market at the time was flexible enough to enable me to spend a minimum of three months away every year and still earn an income that would finance my travels.

Now, at forty-five, I have spent a reasonable amount of time in all continents except Antarctica. I have settled in a few countries for as long as three years. Although I squeezed an anthropology degree in among my travels, I can honestly say that traveling taught me more than my academic studies ever did.

How To Use This Book

When I thought about writing this book I asked myself, "What would have been helpful to know or do in order to travel well when I first started? How could I have enhanced my learning? How could I have planned my nomadic life with ease? How could I have learned to deal with obstacles before and during my trip?" I have made mistakes I could have avoided if I spent more time on planning, or if I simply knew how to adjust when slipping away from my original idea. I have tried to use what I have learned to help you avoid the same mistakes.

However, this is not simply a book revealing a planning method. It is important to discover your own style since everyone's is different. In my case, I spent years looking at other people on the road and trying to copy what they were doing. While this works to a certain degree on practical things, it can be a recipe for disaster if you do not know in advance whether the things you are copying agree with your personality, your likes and dislikes, as well as your beliefs and values.

For instance, you might decide on a destination based on the fact that you have a dear friend there who raves about it. Once you get there, you might discover that your assumptions were wrong, and that the things your friend loves about the place are not the things that are important to you. Do you think a little planning would have helped you? You can bet on it.

After reading this book , you will know clearly what questions you should have asked your friend in advance. You will also learn to dig deeper, to look for the beauty and the magic of traveling as a tool for self-discovery; you will uncover how to better overcome adversities and how to always come out on top, and you will find a place within yourself where there is peace and balance.

The first chapter of this book starts with an important exercise to help you get to know yourself, even before we get into any further information. Once you complete this exercise, how you proceed is up to you. It might take you a while to read this book, working through the exercises as you go. Or you might read it all faster by choosing to do the remainder of the exercises later (all the exercises are in the appendix together with a reminder of some questions you might ask yourself).

You will not find research papers or studies to back up my opinions and points of view. This is a nomad guide; we learn by seeing, observing, and living. Once we experience something deep down, we end up with an undeniable, innermost knowing—a teaching meant to be shared with other like-minded souls.

In many cases, as I traveled, the lessons I needed would come at just the right time, as if by magic. This wisdom came from many teachers— the people I met, my good and bad experiences, or simply the ways that I felt when seeing a new place for the first time. I represent these many sources of wisdom with a figure I call "The Magician," who appears throughout this book to share with you the insight and advice he gave me during my travels.

I have condensed this guide to make it short and sweet. There is certainly more to be said about the topics I touch upon here, but my goal is for you to read this and put a workable plan into action now.

Since I assume your goal is to achieve your travel dream quickly, let's start by finding out what you are like, what your dreams are, what is currently stopping you, and how to overcome it.

Chapter 1

How to find Who you Are

"Be the change you want to see in the world."
Gandhi

The Magician welcome:

"The best journey you could ever take is to be on your own. When no one else is around, you can see yourself in your uniqueness, revealing your heart's most noble desires. Do not be scared to live life as yourself! Whatever your true nature, never be ashamed to let it go free. You might travel and enjoy what it gives, then return home one day and find that what you were looking for has always been there, you just could not see it before. That is why you must take the journey now."

Let's start with your why

Many people envision "traveling the world" as something they would love to do; it is penciled into many bucket lists.

For most of us, this dream seems a distant one. But if you are reading this book, chances are you don't want to wait until retirement to start traveling. I hope I can show younger readers how to travel inexpensively and to take advantage of their relative freedom. To some middle-aged readers, as well as seniors, I would like to prove that waiting is mostly unnecessary. I personally consider time to be your most valuable asset, and having met countless people on the road who whined, "I wish I had started sooner!" motivates me to help you stop delaying a possibly life-changing traveling career indefinitely. All of your reasons for waiting may be valid ones, but they can be conquered. As the old proverb says, "The best time to plant a tree is twenty years ago. The second-best time is now."

Without an orientating map (and I don't mean a geographical one), figuring out the steps to take seems an arduous effort. When we are faced with obstacles regarding finances, time, and personal commitments, it is easy to give up. The dream falls like a house of cards because it lacks a solid foundation. While this book as a whole serves this purpose to make you stronger in your determination to travel, this chapter deals with the first step: creating the personal map that will keep you on course.

In this chapter, you will:

- Find your reasons for traveling
- Learn how you can overcome obstacles
- Define your traveling style.

Muscles need to be challenged in order to grow. Similarly, we gain confidence when we deal with a difficult situation. What if I challenge you to start getting closer to your dream right now and to do this exercise? It's time to get your traveling muscles to do some work! The exercise will take about 40 minutes and is a fun, creative endeavor that you can go back to whenever you are trying to achieve something. It's best to start this exercise without preconceptions, so I will explain how this works after the exercise itself.

For this, you will need:

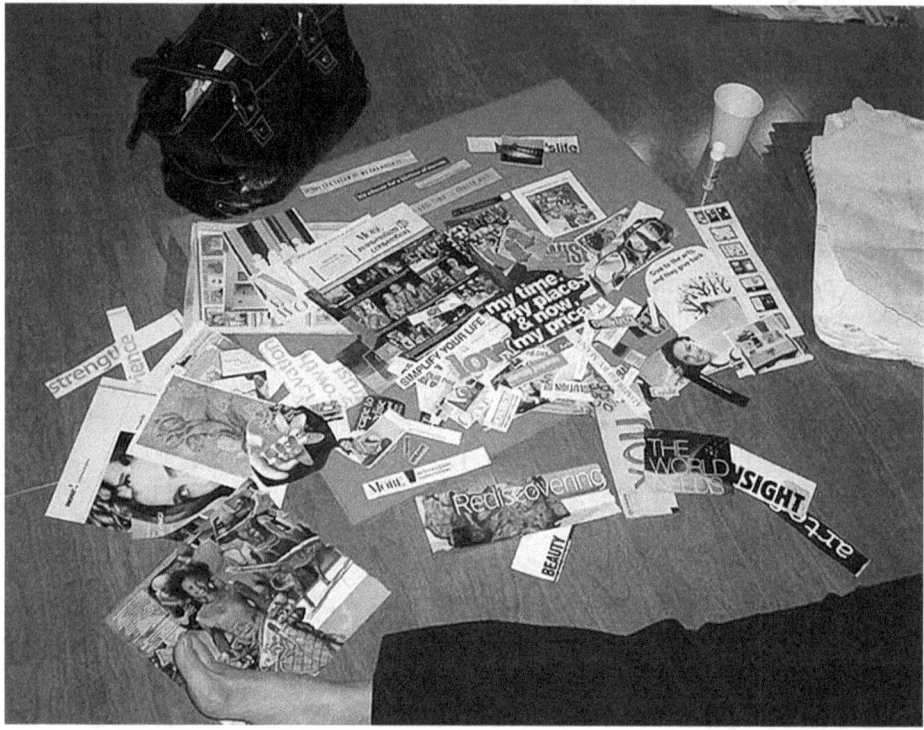

1. An Internet connection
2. A browsing device (tablet or laptop)
3. Access to printing
4. Posterboard (or any large piece of cardboard)
5. Clear tape, pins, or non-permanent glue (such as spray mounting adhesive)
6. Pens or markers

Dreamboard exercise

First, lay out all your supplies (and make sure you have paper in your printer!). Sit comfortably and close your eyes. Now, take several deep breaths, imagining that each exhale carries away your stress and worries, and that each inhale brings you peace and relaxation. When you feel more relaxed, begin the exercise:

1. Begin by asking yourself, "Where have I always wanted to go?" Very simply, try to imagine whichever destination comes to you first. Gather some images in your head.

2. Repeat step 1 for three or four destinations. Try to enjoy the process; record in your head the pleasant sensations and feelings you might experience. Don't rush it! Spend a minimum of ten minutes enjoying your dream destinations, elaborating on the details. Maybe you see a house or a forest nearby, maybe a boat or a train.

Open your eyes and pick up your Internet browsing device. Your job is to find as many similar pictures as you can for the next fifteen minutes. Be creative with your keywords. Search not just the destination's name, but also the words that remind you of the feelings you were experiencing or the settings that you saw, i.e. the type of tree, lake, field, mountain, river and so forth. The images you find might be of specific places, people you saw, situations you imagined, or types of environment. Each time you find an image that matches your imagined destinations, send it to the printer or save it on your device to print later.[1]

Tip: *If you use Google to search for your keywords, try clicking "Images" at the top of the search results page. You'll see pages of images related to your search, plus some general categories that might help you look further.*

---

[1] *To get a screen shot using your keyboard, find below some links to "how to" videos. But beware: sometimes the method depends on the operating system you are using, so if it does not work for you, keep looking for an instructional video that does, as it is bound to be there.*

   https://www.youtube.com/watch?v=EoTplYLBtKs
   (The video above is from Howcast, a reputable channel providing "how-to" tutorials on many topics. Consider making note of it for future use)

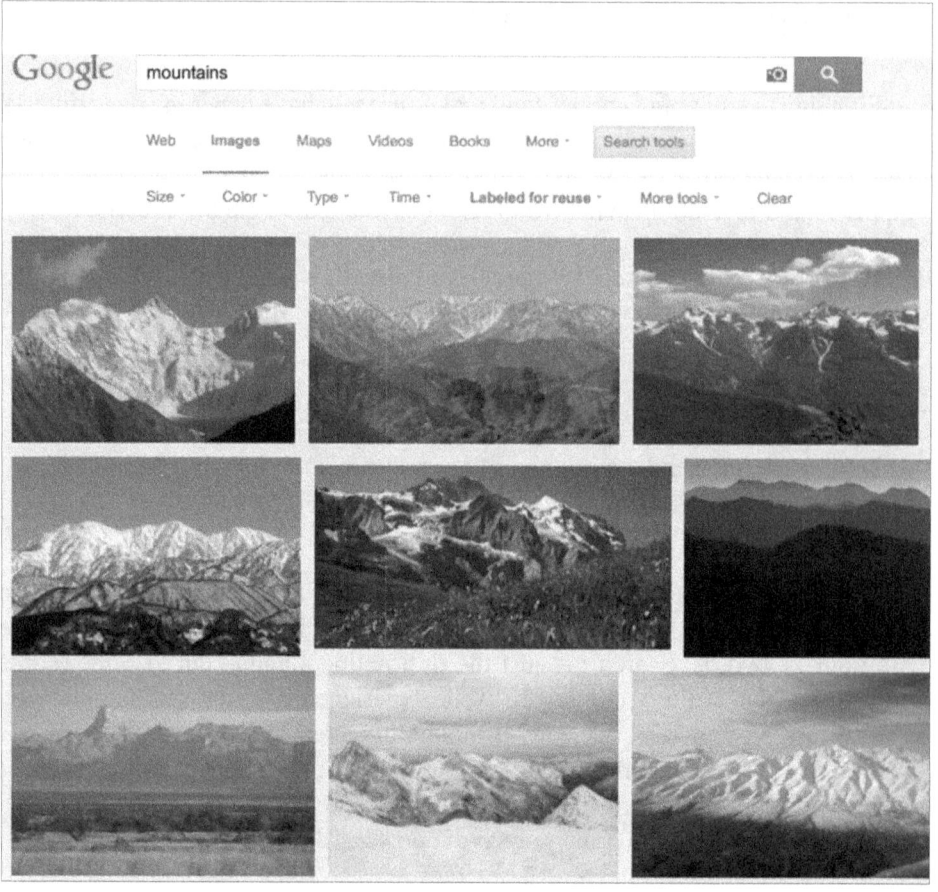

3. Once you have a gallery of destination images, it's time to close your eyes. Breathe deeply and relax as you did previously. When you feel ready, ask yourself the following:

   "While traveling to these places, what would I like to experience?"
   i.e. meet locals, stress-free environments, slow pace, get away from it all, and so forth

   Let it flow for ten minutes, then go back to the Internet and work the same way with your new answers. Try to choose pictures that make a statement, suggest particular experiences, or simply talk to you. Consider searching for quotations that sum up how you felt or would like to feel. You can take a screenshot, print these quotations, or copy them out using colored pens or markers.

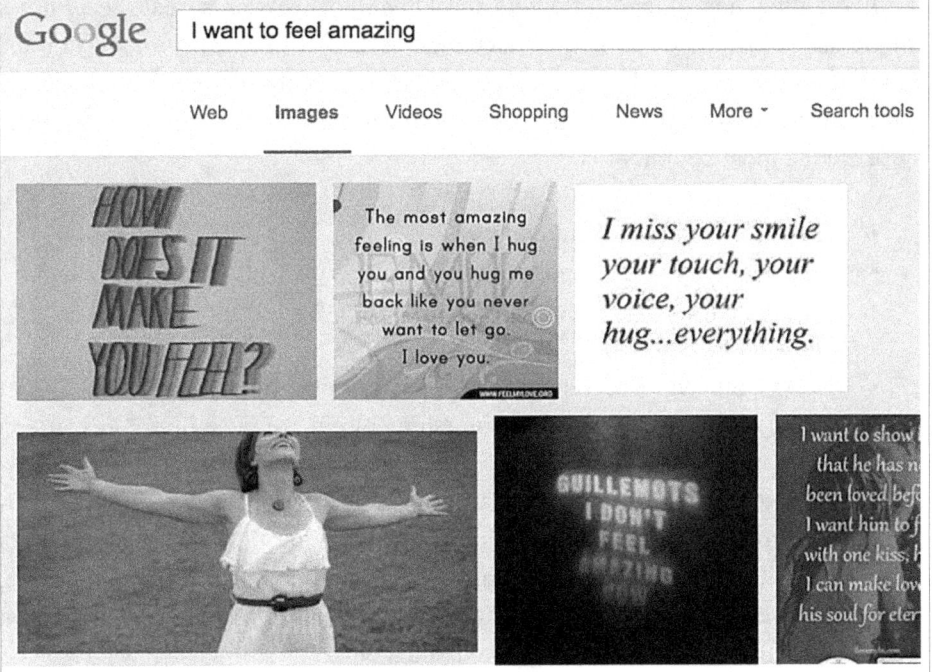

4. Now, look at all of your images. Choose the ones that stand out to you the most, even if you don't know why.

5. Lay your final group of images out on your available board space. Find a way to stick the images onto your board while making sure they are removable (so you can move them around or change them if you feel like it.)

6. Great! Your travel Dreamboard is ready. Post it somewhere you will be sure to see it, such as your bedroom or kitchen. (Some find the bathroom to be the perfect contemplation space!)

Now the difficult bit:

7. Sit in front of your Dreamboard for ten minutes every day. Commit to it! Take it seriously! Gaze at the images for the first five minutes, then close your eyes and spend another five minutes dreaming about your future trip.

Explaining how deeply effective the Dreamboard exercise can be is not a simple task. A friend of mine introduced me to it after he used it to envision the house of his dreams. I took it seriously and have used it myself ever since. I always end up learning something each time I give it a go. It works on various levels; these are the most common:

- Get clear what you want and why
- Get clear why you are not getting it
- Stimulate the mind to come up with ideas
- Keep on track
- Learn / uncover / become aware of any possible limiting beliefs
- Learn if your desire shifts to something else more meaningful to you

Before we go on, consider this: it is universal to believe we all have non-realized dreams. Often we start moving towards them and then give up or get sidetracked. More often, we never even start because we think they are unrealistic, or because we believe we are missing the prerequisites to make them happen (often doubting our personal ability to pursue them).

Most of the time, these beliefs are simply not true. They are limiting thoughts we wrongly address as ultimate truths. I say this because when coaching people, I find that achieving our desires is mostly a matter of developing a strategy that works for the given circumstances, context, and time.

A working strategy: Find out your "Why".

PART ONE: EXERCISE EXPLANATION

It is easy to misconstrue the Dreamboard exercise and to consider it to be not very serious. In reality, the Dreamboard is one of the most powerful tools to achieve any goal, and I will explain why.

We don't have space here for a full class on behavioral psychology, so let me simply tell you there are patterns of experience that determine or influence human behaviors. To a certain extent, we are quite a predictable species. Advertising agencies know this and use specific methods to make us more receptive to subliminal messages or conditioning to promote their brands. Media channels and politicians alike use similar concepts to influence your behaviors.

There are three steps involved in this process:

1) Attention

2) Desire

3) Action

When you watch a commercial for the first time, you might not consciously notice the brand or the product name. But advertisers know that repeating the same slogan or image will bring it to your attention, even at a very low level. They also use images that give us pleasurable sensations: bright colors, attractive people, beautiful scenery. Even if you are not aware of it, some feelings are evoked watching the ad, even if the commercial is in the background.

In the future, when you need a certain product or service, you will be drawn to the brand that is most familiar, especially if it brings up pleasant associations. The ad will succeed if it has imprinted the brand somewhere in your mind, hopefully influencing related purchases in the near future.

None of these mental associations happen on a conscious level. They are more subliminal, reaching the subconscious first before eventually manifesting as a conscious behavior. Psychology theorizes the subconscious is in the driving seat of our behavior. So when the media bypasses our conscious mind (first by showing us a product and then by associating it with pleasurable sensations), they are influencing our future choices, decisions, and behaviors. Unless we are unaware of that influence, we may believe that the desire we feel for that new car is our own.

So, why not reverse-engineer these methods to find out what you *really* desire and make it happen?

Just like an advertisement, the Dreamboard associates visual cues with pleasurable emotional states, as if you have created your own ads, slogans and punch lines. In the Dreamboard exercise, you have envisioned or elaborated on a current dream or goal. You have stimulated pleasurable sensations and feelings while visualizing your goal in your mind's eye. You have chosen "trigger" images that reinforce the association between your goal and those pleasurable feelings, and you have put the images on a Dreamboard where they can serve as a constant physical reminder.

Now we could leave it there, just a collage hanging somewhere in your house; this would simply reflect your desire for travel. But if you look at it every day, its images will over time activate a psychological desire for your goal. The desire will be much stronger each time you pay more attention to it, so that it can eventually be experienced on a conscious level too.

PART TWO: DEEPENING QUESTION

Now that you have a sense of *what* you want when you travel, I invite you to discover something profound by asking yourself the following question: *"Why do I want to travel?"*

Finding your "why" is very revealing. Once you know the real reason, the passion behind your desire for travel, you will have discovered your biggest ally in making your dream a reality.

Some "why" examples could be: fun, inspiration, change, lifestyle, or adventure. I suggest that you do not stop there. Instead, elaborate your answer further. For instance, saying, "I would like to travel because I get inspired by it," doesn't express what exactly inspires you.

Let yourself imagine being inspired. What will your insight be? Will you realize a specific quality? Develop a new attitude? Don't worry if the answer is not clear at first-- it will become clearer the more time you spend with the question.

Even if after all the thinking you have done you come up with a simple answer, such as, "I want to travel because I just want to," that is fine! Imagination is more powerful than concepts or words, and some people are more visual than others. Spend time imagining travel scenarios with all the fun and joy associated with them. Focus on the images flooding your mind, using them to replace words.

In The Appendix, you will find a section giving you more ideas about why you might want to travel, but try to come up with your unique answers first.

The Magician's advice:

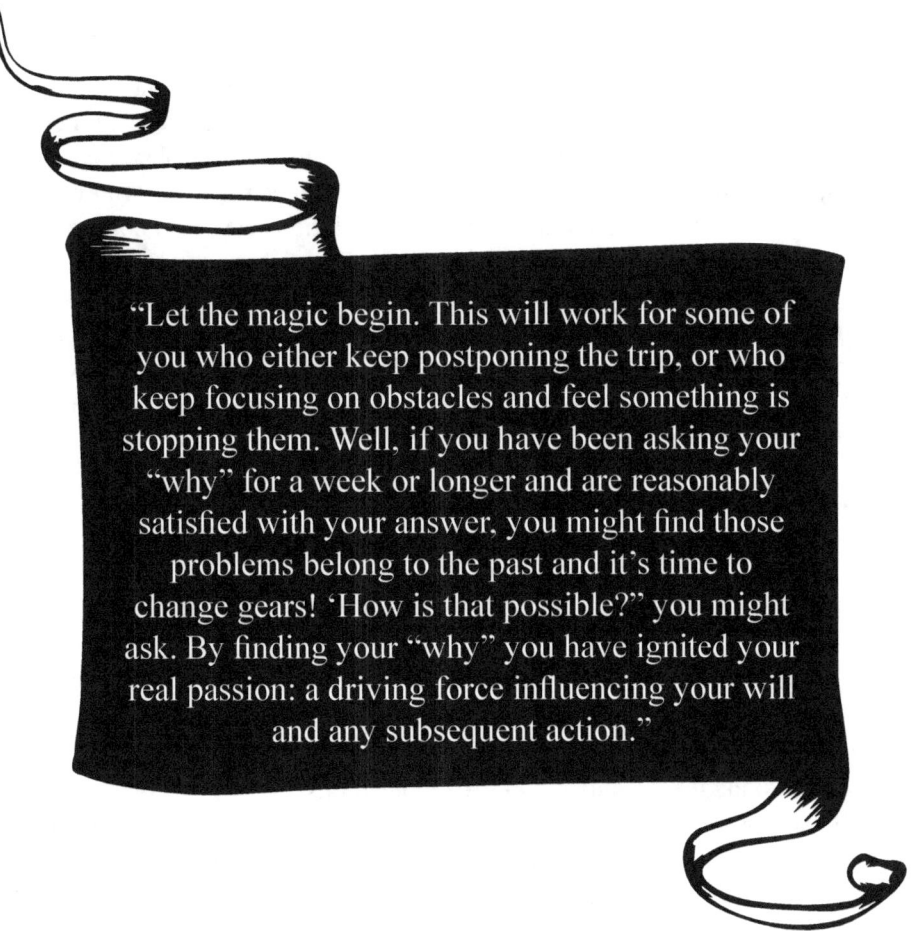

"Let the magic begin. This will work for some of you who either keep postponing the trip, or who keep focusing on obstacles and feel something is stopping them. Well, if you have been asking your "why" for a week or longer and are reasonably satisfied with your answer, you might find those problems belong to the past and it's time to change gears! 'How is that possible?'" you might ask. By finding your "why" you have ignited your real passion: a driving force influencing your will and any subsequent action."

PART THREE: OVERCOMING OBSTACLES

Let's look at what is currently keeping you from fulfilling your travel dreams. Here is a list of the most common reasons:
- Lack of financial savings
- Lack of time (i.e. vacation from work)
- Uncertainty about destinations
- Fear of traveling alone
- Conflicting partner commitments

Your obstacles may be quite daunting at first, seeming very difficult to overcome. After posing the "why" question, you may find that your perspective on your obstacles is now different, and you start finding ways to solve them. They might even start to look more like excuses than real reasons.

What has happened is that we have added some new resources-- through desire and pleasure-- to make us more congruent with our innermost strengths. We took the time to grow them, so now we are ready to face our obstacles. In other words, each time we think of our challenges and problems, we now have enough breathing space in our minds to come up with solutions we could not see before.

Take finances, for instance. We may not find enough money because we don't have a dedicated account to which we commit to deposit into regularly. We need to implement strategies to help us buy less useless stuff. Why not create a saving strategy for travel? To do this, we can assess how we spend money currently, divide our spending into categories, and make a spreadsheet. Once the data is collected, we can then ask:

- "Is our spending out of control?"
- "Can we save more?"
- "Can we cut expenses"
- "Can we spend less?"
- "Can we earn more?"

You then can compile a list of specific actions you can take in each of those areas, helping you with the "how." I will give more ideas in Chapter 3; for now, consider asking the question, "Do I really need this?"

If the answer is no, maybe you can contribute that money to your travel account instead. I really hope that by the time you have finished reading this book, you will feel resourceful enough to come up with several income generation ideas. Putting them to use as your travel progresses will establish confidence in your ability to solve any money blockages and fears you might still hold onto.

Now consider a relationship commitment. You might be in a position to ignite passion in your partner, who will either join you or give you the okay simply because your words about traveling will reveal how important this is for you.

Similarly, you may handle negotiating time off from work with more conviction and persuasion. You may even feel so strongly that you decide to quit!

What if your obstacle is fear? Maybe you have never traveled. Or maybe you have, but it was a disaster. In that case, remind yourself that the past is not equal to the future; if you have traveled before with bad results, you might use that experience to your own advantage.

Sometimes we may fear a specific scenario. What if we had some control over that scenario? Using the power of imagination and a technique called Neuro-

Linguistic Programming (NLP),[2] we can work on a specific fear and obliterate it. For the scope of this book, I have designed a process (appendix 2) that may help.

Don't anticipate disaster; why not expect some kind of adventure instead? I recently took a short vacation with a friend who is not used to traveling. Just hours before the flight, she twisted her ankle.

Even though she would not have full mobility, she still did not let the injury interfere with her plans to enjoy the holiday. A fearful person would not have envisioned such a possibility; perhaps such a person would have postponed or canceled the trip altogether. Instead, limping her way between wheel chairs and local hospitals abroad, she had an awesome time.

If you fear injury during travel, try imagining yourself still enjoying the vacation with such an injury. In fact, the difference between having the same kind of injury at home or abroad can simply be all in your head. What if being overseas and healing in the sunshine might be an even better scenario than healing in familiar surroundings at home?

This is how creative I invite you to be. Develop an attitude of saying "yes," a willingness to overcome fears and to embrace obstacles. Be like a child who falls when learning to walk; a child keeps trying, so why do you want to give up? How important is travel to you? Finding these answers will make you determined to succeed and relentless, even unstoppable, in your pursuits!

Even though you are getting more motivated to pursue your dream, it is not yet time to define it. Instead, let's find out more of who you are by thinking about your traveling style.

Will You Find Flow?

There are many ways to travel, and it is certainly possible to keep adjusting and switching between what I call "traveling styles." This book is about a traveling lifestyle that can be either part-time or full-time; you could take a trip lasting a few months, years, or simply go nomadic.

While most people can easily achieve temporary breaks, going nomadic is a

---

[2] *Neuro-linguistic programming (NLP) is a psychotherapeutic modality created by Richard Bandler and John Grinder in the 70's. Robert Dilt, (the primary contributor to NLP) states that " NLP stands for Neuro-Linguistic Programming, a name that encompasses the three most influential components involved in producing human experience: neurology, language and programming. The neurological system regulates how our bodies function, language determines how we interface and communicate with other people and our programming determines the kinds of models of the world we create. Neuro-Linguistic Programming describes the fundamental dynamics between mind (neuro) and language (linguistic) and how their interplay affects our body and behavior (programming)" http://www.nlpu.com/NewDesign/NLPU_WhatIsNLP.html*

gradual process and doesn't happen to many people overnight. Even while on the road, many like to find places to settle temporarily. On your first trip, though, this is not necessarily what you might prefer to do. Deciding in advance how long you will be away as a part-time nomad, while practical, often interrupts the process that I call "flow" in which most of the benefits of travel can be found.

I suggest people go away for a minimum of one year, and remain flexible enough for an extension (I will give more details of how to plan for this in Chapter 3). If this seems like a long time, consider that it takes at least three months for your accumulated stress to disappear.

We often don't even realize we are stressed in the first place. Travel forces you to let go of all you left behind, and eventually brings you to a point where you become lighter and more cheerful without any alcohol or mind-altering substances! You are simply high on life. After having this kind of experience, the three-week vacation style will no longer make any sense or will simply lose value. Once you make it past three weeks, you will have passed the first test on the road towards becoming a nomad. At this point you will be able to decide if traveling is for you and how it might enrich your experience.

What follows might sound a bit philosophical to some of you. Others might already recognize what I am talking about because it is a kind of experience not exclusive to traveling but is instead something that is shared throughout life in various forms, as I am going to explain a bit later. I consider this a kind of treasure, a life inner-insight in which your heart's desires align with the very moment you are living. It is the footprint you might leave behind, or perhaps your ability to be fully immersed, participating with all of your being in what is in front of you.

When flow is subjectivelly understood, it is like a teacher who is unable to be heard bu us because we are so deep in our logically-operated inner-world that separetes us from the experience we are living.

When we chase material goals, flow stay silent. However flow will be there as soon there is enough space for it to come through.

I refrain from confusing you by adding references to a concept you do not yet recognize, Firsr, let's define it a bit better, and then my own story can clarify it further.

To explain flow, I call forward the Magician:

"Being 'in the flow' means you're going to experience the day-to-day activities with almost no effort. As you travel, the responsibilities you carried from your old life begin to fade. Your psyche begins to be fueled by the experience. This mental state gives you more courage to try things and awakens curiosity for the new. Walking this unknown territory fills your life with awe. Of course, while you will experience this to different degrees, be asssured that it will happen at one point and can be very cathartic. You will be tempted to reevaluate your entire life, make new goals, set new ambitions for yourself, and embrace new beliefs. There is no way to make flow last forever, but once experienced, the absence of tension and stress will naturally enable everything you learn to integrate into the new you. You might talk and act differently as a result of having been in flow. You can experience it consciously or unconsciously; it's up to you. The rewards will be always living life while fulfilling your innermost desires and behaving in a manner much more congruent to your own values."

After I finished my schooling in London (where I'd moved to brush up on my English), I took a gap year. As a kid brought up on a diet of Eastern mysticism, I had only one destination in mind: Asia, specifically India and Indonesia.

My port of entry was New Delhi, and the culture shock was unbelievable. I moved around a lot in the beginning; from the Himalayas, I followed the holy river Ganges all the way to Varanasi, the city of death. The trip took me a few months. I kept a journal, amazed by everything my mind was recording. The things I saw were so different from what I'd known that any attempt to interpret them was futile. Yet, they made me reevaluate many things I had taken for granted.

The real trigger for my own flow experience was a humbling lesson taught by a beggar, who gave me money when I had none. How could this be? I had thought most poor Indians saw westerners as an opportunity to gain some money, or at least perceived them to be rich. Instead, here was a barefoot old man, wearing nothing but a dirty, ripped robe who recognized another human being struggling and offered what little he had to help. This event was enough to jolt me into a new perspective in which I renegotiated my worldview with myself.

Until then, I had functioned according to old patterns, being distant and fearful, always analyzing, evaluating, and acting responsibly. At that crossroads, I opened up instead. For the first time, I saw what was in front of me. The secular Indian reality no longer seemed so foreign or backwards. Differences in skin color, culture, and religion were no longer impenetrable. When we shift the focus from our diversities to our similarities, we see that the human experience is much more shareable than we might have thought.

From then on, I communicated differently. No longer counting on language alone, I took advantage of facial expression, gestures, and touch. I found a way of communicating without wearing armor to hide my vulnerability, clumsiness, and inadequacy. I became wholly transparent, and this began to define my traveling style. Many times I heard myself saying, "I did not know I had it in me" when I suddenly opened up, tapping into the energy of a kid by embracing new playful and enriching experiences. Living less in my mind enabled me to learn to immensely enjoy being in the "now."

I have included this story so you can begin to see how profound the experience of flow can be. Once you reach a state of flow, of openness, traveling can become addictive because it provides you with a constant opportunity to grow, educate, learn, and experience vibrant and colorful cultures almost as an insider.

This might seem idealistic to some--for instance, to those who find themselves in a career mindset and work far too much, missing out. My hope is that you are open enough not to be too cynical so this description can inspire you to take your next trip for a longer period of time.

I won't deny it, people can find flow within their profession as well. Contemporary psychologist Csikszentmihalyi- who firstly refers to flow as an ecstatic experience necessary in the pursuit of happiness- based his observation on artists and workers who perfected their crafts effortlessly completely absorbed in the task rather than consciously doing it. While Csikszentmihalyi defines his theory on the deepening of specific life passions, abilities, and vocations in order to experience flow, here instead the base (or departing point) is quite different.

During traveling, the mind is bombarded with new experiences and its job of interpreting and attributing meaning becomes futile as it lacks past references. Eventually this causes the mind to become flexible in those mechanics, although instead of plunging in total confusion an ecstatic state is reached. The main difference between the two approaches is that flow is to be also an altered pleasurable mental state which comes not from excelling at something but rather from having failed, through common sense and reason, to adjust to life on the road. Besides that, the flow experience is almost identical to what Csikszentmihalyi theorizes, despite differences in its triggers. The total immersion in the experience, that Csikszentmihalyi describes, is also what is experienced by the traveler. This will happen eventually-- it all depends on the individual's emotional predisposition, as some people could be resistant and keep defending their emotional states. Flow is "total," as it requires considerable emotional openness to come through. If the person is fully immersed in something they like and they know how to do, they tend to be already open. Below is a slide from one of Csikszentmihalyi's lectures:

HOW DOES IT FEEL TO BE IN FLOW

1. Completely involved in what we are doing – focused, concentrated.
2. A sense of ecstasy – of being outside everyday reality.
3. Great inner clarity – knowing what needs to be done, and how well we are doing.
4. Knowing that the activity is doable – that our skills are adequate to the task.
5. A sense of serenity – no worries about oneself, and a feel of growing beyond the boundaries of the ego.
6. Timelessness – thoroughly focused on the present, hours seem to pass by in minutes.
7. Intrinsic motivation – whatever produces flow becomes its own reward.

Instead, the nomad, could be quite fearful at first, making the dynamic of flow less easy to experience. Travel is always challenging, but only extended travel will test you until you surrender to the experience. Give yourself enough time to reach that state of flow where you can enjoy all aspects of a wondrous life with no fixed address, no security, few rules, and no responsibilities.

Everyone is unique; so is flow. It is an inner experience, like an initiation or a coming-of-age ritual. You'll know when you reach a peak with your flow experience. You will feel in your gut that something has changed; you might not even have the words for it, and you might shed a tear or two. Your understanding of flow might not be immediate or have any clarity, so set your compass by the intensity of your emotions; that is your peak!

This poem can help you understand how to be, even if the experience of your peak is not a pleasurable one (remember that pain can also be a great teacher).

The Guest House

This being human is a guest house.
Every morning a new arrival.
A joy, a depression, a meanness,
some momentary awareness comes
as an unexpected visitor.

Welcome and entertain them all!
Even if they're a crowd of sorrows,
who violently sweep your house
empty of its furniture,
still, treat each guest honorably.
He may be clearing you out for some new delight.

The dark thought, the shame, the malice
meet them at the door laughing,
and invite them in.

Be grateful for whoever comes,
because each has been sent as a guide from beyond.

Rumi.

In this chapter, we dreamt of distant destinations. We considered complicated concepts regarding how the mind works, and thought about strategies to remove obstacles and fears. We have briefly touched on the concept of "flow"-- do not worry if you don't quite understand what flow is yet, as you will know what it is once you feel it. In the next chapter, we will explore more about traveling styles and determine where you fit in.

2

Traveling Styles

"Normal is getting dressed in clothes that you buy for work and driving through traffic in a car that you are still paying for, in order to get to the job you need to pay for the clothes and the car, and the house you leave vacant all day so you can afford to live in it."
Ellen Goodman

What the Magician likes to point out…

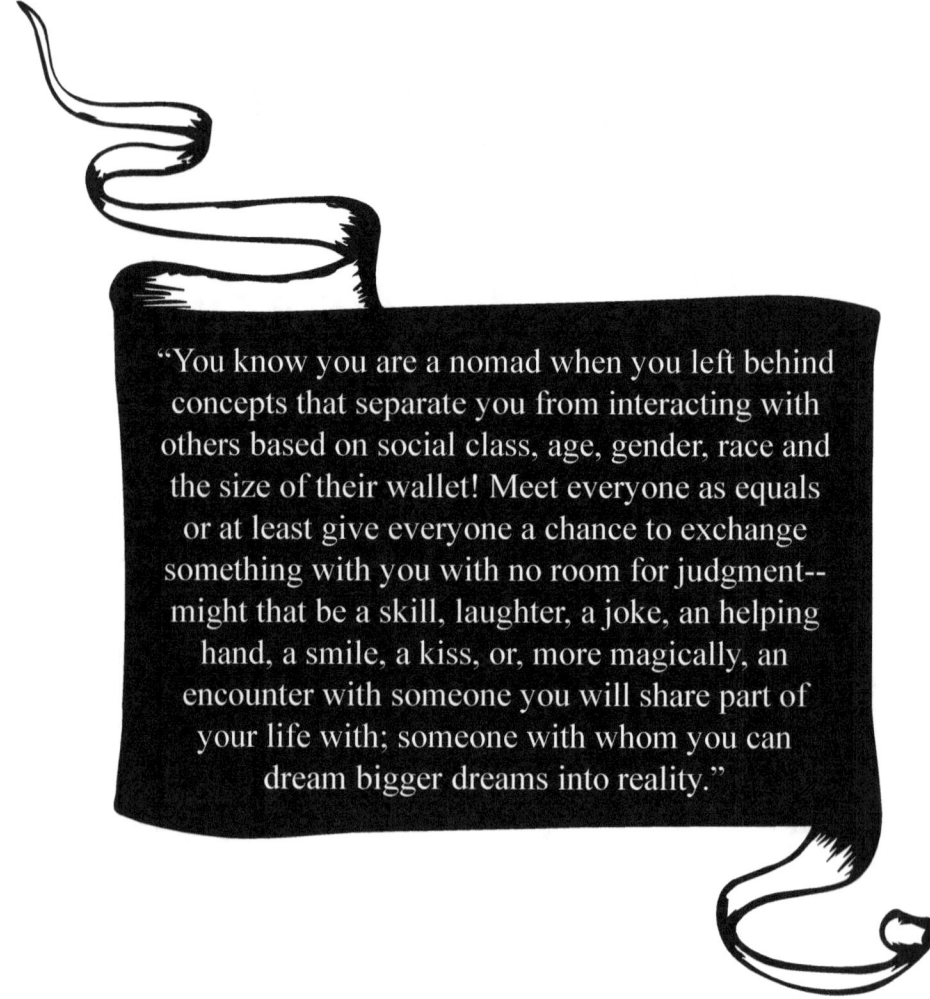

"You know you are a nomad when you left behind concepts that separate you from interacting with others based on social class, age, gender, race and the size of their wallet! Meet everyone as equals or at least give everyone a chance to exchange something with you with no room for judgment-- might that be a skill, laughter, a joke, an helping hand, a smile, a kiss, or, more magically, an encounter with someone you will share part of your life with; someone with whom you can dream bigger dreams into reality."

Below I will give you three traveling style scenarios based on age, background, and experience.

You can mix and match them as you please in order to determine which is more applicable to you. However, bear in mind that once you are in flow, your style might change as you overcome previously held limitations and fears. These three examples are a foundation. Although extremely basic, they apply to a beginner nomad and can be used as a reference. I invite you to reflect on these basic levels, on which you can later build on as you progressively adjust to life on the road.

Traveling will give you variety and adventure, each day different from the last. This is the perfect scenario to find your passion and what you really like to do. This will not only help you in traveling, but it will also make you more authentic, defining you as a person.

As children, we loved to play, and that is also how we learned. The problem started when adults said "no" to us. Most of the time, this form of conditioning is in the hands of our parents, others close relatives, and schooling. Sometimes they even shouted at us: "No! Don't do that!"

Many times, the adults around us said "no" to protect us. But sometimes, the adults were simply fearful or angry, and said "no" to our natural curiosity and enthusiasm in order to control us. I call these adults "dream crushers", destroying any precious dreams and passions-- our very soul essence.

Once our dreams are crushed, later on in life we forget we even had passion and ambitions to begin with. Take the opportunity now to reconnect with those, wh seeing if you can recognize a bit of yourself in any of these styles.

Scenario one: Wild, Young and Free

This group has the following traits:

- Adaptable/ flexible
- Requires less comfort
- Fun and orientated
- Fast-paced
- Not so serious
- Doubtful
- Plans change often
- Not very resourceful
- Not so conscientious
- Active

Archetypically symbolized by the "gap-year backpacker," this style is not limited to age. Plenty of middle-aged people adopt this style with a few variations. For instance, the need for more comfortable accommodations may increase with age, although this is not always the case.

If you are young, it is most likely you don't have much traveling experience, unless you grew up in a traveling Mecca (such as Goa), or if your parents have been on the road. Youth can be an advantage, as you will be more flexible and can adapt to change very quickly. You will absorb the learning provided by the traveling school as if you were a sponge.

All young people respond well to discoveries and new experiences. The problem is that things can get too wild. If that happens, you might be unaware of your flow.

Although you might make several such free-style trips, even the typical "gap-year traveler" knows deep down that they are eventually going back to life at home. So, this addictive, fun-orientated traveling style comes with a "sell-by date" by which all experiences are limited. This style of flow can be summed up with the romantic motto, "You only live once." Nobody can tell this kind of young traveler otherwise; they can only change their minds from within. If what I just said holds some truth for you, you'll thrive on the road. You might turn challenges into a lot of fun, and even if things go catastrophically wrong, this experience will be a valuable teacher in learning about your limits.

I lived for a few years in Ibiza, a party island in southern Spain. I'll tell you, living there made me aware that plenty of people in their sixsties and seventies (or even older) haven't stopped partying, embodying extreme hedonism as their flow.

Naturally, a younger person will gravitate towards fun-oriented destinations. Thailand and Southeast Asia in general can accommodate a low budget really well. While you may not find the hippie dream-world island depicted in the novel "The Beach" by Alex Garland (also a cult motion picture starring Leonardo Di Caprio), you will meet plenty of people with a free-spirited mindset. Being lost in a maze of crazy destinations allows for a multitude of "daze days.": bonding rituals, sleepless nights, days spent in a twilight zone- - all of which will challenge your traveling plans.

While I was in Indonesia, I fell in with a group of travelers. One night, we began to discuss a possible three-day hike of a volcano, Mount Rinjani, on the island of Lombok. As the evening progressed, we all got very drunk; in this heated state, we made the decision to set sail for Lombock the following day in order to start our adventure. The boat to take us there was scheduled to depart at 10:00 am. Still, we danced until dawn before departing for our respective guesthouses. The following morning, I had to pack everything and go. Needless to say, I almost missed the boat. When I arrived at the shore, one of those old-fashioned, long-tail fishing boats with winged edges was already sailing away. Seventeen of my fellow intrepid adventurers were happily on board. Luckily they made the boat turn back around when they spotted me on the coral sand, waving at them in desperation.

Little did I know that this trip was going to represent a monumental shift for me in terms of facing many of my travel fears. It was my first ever multi-day hike, and not an easy one either. Three days on a volcano turned into three weeks of traveling in the Nusa Tenggara archipelago with a diverse group of people in terms of age, backgrounds, and even continents of origin. As difficult as the terrain could be, the trip gave me the opportunity to bond deeply with the other participants. I remained friends with some of them for years- - and this was before the Internet and mobile phones, when people without fixed abodes were difficult to track!

Eat & Sleep

Younger travelers generally need to stretch their money in order to make it last as long as possible. This means living on a shoestring budget, especially when choosing where to eat or sleep. Low-budget travel means adapting to less comfortable accommodations, which sometimes even lean towards the Spartan and somewhat unhygienic.

Bedbugs are the traveler's nightmare. They itch like crazy and stay with you for a while after you get bitten. If you are unfortunate enough to sleep on a mattress infested with them, you can use antihistamine tablets to deal with this inconvenience. If you suspect bedbugs, keep all of your luggage and other possessions in plastic garbage bags so the bugs won't catch a ride home with you.

Hostels are low-budget accommodations that vary from place to place in terms of standards. Once you have experienced a modern "boutique hostel," though, it's hard to go back. They can be quite luxurious, boasting very comfortable beds and amenities. However, the beauty of traveling on a low budget is realizing soon enough that you don't need much. A basic room begins to look a lot better after you have slept in it for a few days. You might be calling it home after a month, as living standards adapt at a great speed.

Food also can also be surprisingly varied and cheap. You can find new and interesting flavors to explore by eating where the locals eat. I was on the banks of the Nile River in Egypt recently, and although I had a good budget, I chose to eat at local places in order to have a more authentic experience.

You may hear warnings about local food making travelers sick, and certainly new foods, unfamiliar spices, and differences in standards of cleanliness can lead to an upset stomach. Over time, however, you will become more experienced and selective about where you eat, and the chances of getting sick from local food will be slim. The real threat may be choosing to eat western foods in places where they are not normally eaten. Chances are, the turnaround on these foods is not high, and eating food that is not fresh is the real culprit when people get food poisoning. Eating the regional food is a safer bet most of the time.

Before you travel, research fasting and other natural ways to detox, as well as the kinds of parasites travelers may come across and what to do about them. (More on this in Chapter 6.)

Activities & Lifestyle

Having a youthful, fun-orientated approach will enable people to turn most activities into playful ones; there tend to be a lot of thrill seekers in this group. For instance, ducking tree branches while riding on the crowded rooftop of a bus and going at treacherous speeds might turn out to be a joyful activity. Sharing your space with chicken, pigs, sheep, or exotic birds might be your idea of feeling free. You might arrive at a destination and hire a WW2 Jeep to cross a minefield--or, even better, to cruise the desert during a storm, zigzagging like a slalom racer to avoid being hit by lightening. You may enjoy swimming in the ocean under the moonlight to experience bioluminescence.[3] Or learning ancient tribal rituals and dances, jumping off cliffs, kayaking in the deep jungle, and trekking to find hidden lagoons and caves. These are exhilarating examples to whet your appetite for adventures. Adrenaline sports, such as white water rafting, can be an attraction for the young, wild, and free, so research your opportunities for adventure before you reach your destination. Here is a list of various types of extremes sports.

http://extremefreestyle.wordpress.com/2008/05/24/list-of-extreme-sports

---

[3] *Bioluminescence (dictionary meaning) Emission of light by an organism or biochemical system It occurs in a wide range of protists and animals, including bacteria and fungi, insects, marine invertebrates, and fish. In this case I refer to protozoa, commonly found in tropical seas. (concise Dictionary)*

TRAVELING STYLES

The lifestyle of younger travelers can be hectic; they may move around a lot, trying to reach as many destinations as possible. However, trying to accomplish too many things in a short time can work against you. Pace yourself-- traveling gets tiring, so schedule some breaks between destinations, even when you are young.

There is a risk that young travelers might not take obstacles, challenges, and problems seriously. This could be attributed to a lack of experience, which allows them to fail to recognize risks, which can be dangerous. People in this group get carried away and are easily excited. Because of this, a single trip that goes well might ignite a passion to become a nomad. However, if things go wrong, a young traveler might become deeply disappointed— so much that the trip becomes a once-in-a-lifetime pursuit, never to be repeated. Young travelers might experience many doubts, frequent changes of plan, and possibly a lot of blackouts and hangovers!

Second scenario: The intrepid middle-aged explorer.

This group has the following characteristics:

- Stable
- Not too wild or adventurous
- Conscientious
- Sticks to plans
- Likes comforts and commodities
- Finds it hard to give up technology
- Chatty
- Generous
- Experienced

Life has many seasons. When middle-age sets in, it comes with a series of achievements and lessons learned. This will mean approaching traveling with maturity and possibly wealth.

Money and wealth have different meanings in different cultures. A very humbling experience is to choose a non-materialist destination for one of your trips. Especially if you measure your self-worth by the size of your wallet and assets, those types of destinations might be helpful. Think of indigenous or tribal cultures with little exposure to and influence from western consumerism or largely not affected by it. If you so choose, stay away from settlements where the indigenous culture is packaged in a "meet-the-native" type tour, where the guide (often local) takes you to meet the native, buy their handmade crafts, eat in their houses, and witness their dances or rituals. There is little authenticity in that if any. Explore the possibility instead of spending some time in such a community, participating, sharing, and learning.

These opportunities are abound in the Andes, Nepal, Laos, the Amazon basin, Ethiopia, and Northern Canada. You don't need to volunteer necessarily, but often you will need a permit from the authorities to visit protected zones. If you do, you'll experience an anthropological perspective enriching your worldview.

This group tends to be more grounded, determined not to waste time. They are more attached to finding a meaning in their trip and wandering around. They are most likely to want to make their life skills useful, or to trade them for learning new ones. Some adapt easily to new environments, always asking themselves how can they fit in. Conversely, others may have a tendency to impose their own ways over the local culture they find themselves in during their journeys.

At some point, with the accumulation of traveling tales under the belt and after stacking moments of bliss upon deep life-learning, there comes a time when all nomads reach a plateau. This is a dreaded time for some nomads. Traveling seems to have lost value, and long gone are the days when you felt in awe of your surroundings, replaced by a sense of utter boredom. This is the time that calls for a breakthrough. You will soon figure out that you need to take a very profound step and feel somehow useful. It is a time to fulfill the human need for contribution. Working as a volunteer or simply taking an active role in helping a local community serves this purpose very well. So, if you ever feel stuck in your travel, consider this possibility as a permanent solution to your problem.

Eat & Sleep

Travel at this age generally calls for higher budgets. Even if you have an unlimited credit card, however, I invite you to think of your greater financial comfort as simply having more choices within your reach. Try to balance wealth with the idea that nomads are not attached to their wealth. They share the pie with total strangers and gravitate towards less fortunate communities where they contribute and bond.

Your Dreamboard destinations might possibly include a tropical paradise. Yachting your way into the Caribbean islands is a style that you could explore, as well as visiting Eco-resorts slotted around the planet. Since your budget allows for this flexibility, you could do just that, finding your flow in that kind of travel would be very revealing. The scenario you pictured yourself in-- dotted with luxuries, commodities, and comfort-- will over time prove to be fragile and extremely sterile. These dreams are short-lived; although enjoyable, they have a sell-by date. The tropical beach becomes less attractive; the coconut palm tree, just a tree; the over-water lagoon bungalows with on-demand amenities gets depressive; the cabin in the yacht, claustrophobic (or worse, considering the rolling motion of the boat!)

After a few months of luxury, it's time to get real!

If you reach the awareness that luxury is not the point of travel, but still want some amenities, you may want to opt for an RV: a mobile home that has always been the symbol for nomadic life. Sometimes costing as much as a house, an RV has the added bonus of coming with wheels. This life can be fun, and RV-ers are a good bunch of people who have alternative perspectives of life and are always keen on helping each other. They are in flow and are most often very resourceful with tons of skills. They are also good at earning a living, as well as trading anything you can think of.

If RV-ing is not an option, or simply not interesting to you, the middle-aged traveler might gravitate eventually towards a more adventurous but slower-paced style of travel. There is a lot of fun to be had mixing with other travelers and locals. They are in a position to rent nice houses and now, with AirBnB and other sites with in-built social networking, it's possible to find very good deals. Second home renters are plentiful, and middle-aged travelers would qualify easily for house-sitting if they don't mind taking up chores such as gardening or pet-minding.

Activities & Lifestyle

This group tends to be more stable and more likely to stick to the plan. They can be single or partnered, and many have kids in home-schooling. Today, this can be easily delivered with e-tutors- all you need is an Internet connection. You will find some e-tutoring resources in the appendix at the end of this book.

This group tends to engage in outdoor and cultural activities. They are less prone to mix with strangers or join in free-spirited parties or similar happenings on a beach with a few beers, guitars, and bonfires.

Activities that members of this group find themselves enjoying time and time again include:
- Hiking
- Camping
- Being in nature
- Bird-watching

- Golf
- Cultural evenings
- Folk festivals
- Soaking in the local culture
- Museum and cultural sites

Middle-aged people have a tendency to be more judgmental. However, this may stop once they discover their flow. One of the challenges this group might face is in meeting younger people with more wisdom than they have. They need to be open enough to learn from younger people who are pros at traveling. The traveling lifestyle is a learned skill, after all, and age is irrelevant. Some young people are extremely gifted. Recognizing them enables you to borrow from their knowledge, which can be very valuable and rewarding. Consider paying or tipping in exchange for acquiring traveling wisdom.

Magician poem:

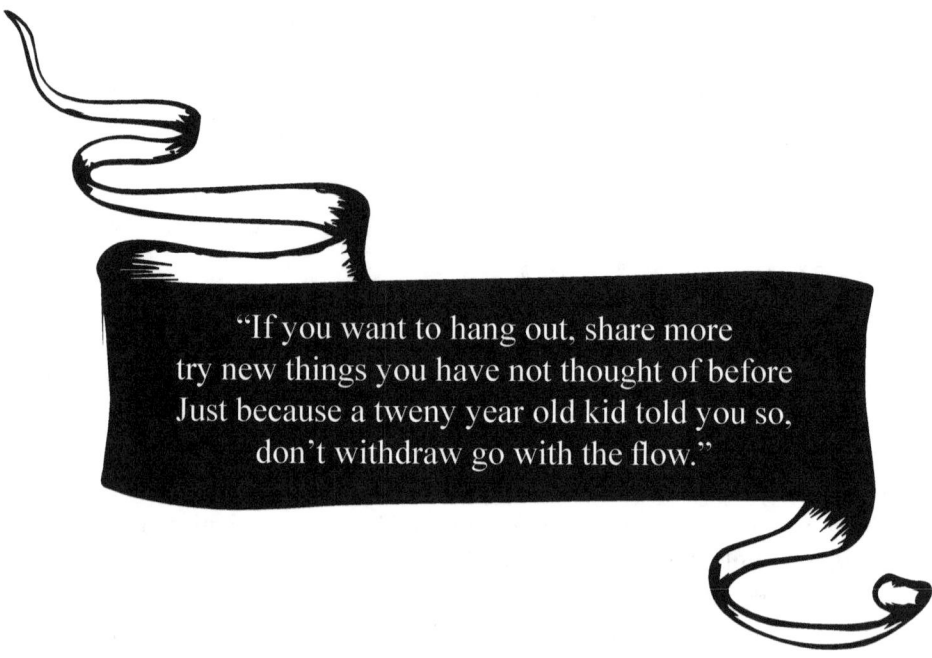

"If you want to hang out, share more
try new things you have not thought of before
Just because a tweny year old kid told you so,
don't withdraw go with the flow."

Third Scenario: Senior's Silver Charm

Traits:

- Less accommodating
- Can be particular at times
- Keeps to him or herself
- Finds it hard to communicate with locals
- Demanding
- Wise
- Can be confident or insecure
- Can be experienced or dependent
- Seeks out safety

This is the most flexible scenario. What you have done all of your life can enrich the traveling community's spirit a great deal. Travel at this age can be fun too, almost as if a new youth is found. Don't be surprised when you meet young people who appreciate you and cherish your company.

Finding flow can be extremely cathartic, and perhaps you will shed a lot of tears in the process. They are good tears though; you have reached your age of wisdom, after all, and the best way to get credit is by traveling. You will have practical opportunities to apply your wisdom and gain much more.

The first challenge for many senior travelers is to become less rigid by practicing better listening skills. You might spend a long time just doing that and learning how it works. Your flow might take longer to find, but you will find it eventually.

Rigidity often translates to saying "no" too often to what life offers you. When traveling, "no" will get you nowhere. You need to learn to say, "Yes!"

Once, I got stuck in Lisbon airport (as my plane was delayed a few hours), so I started to chat with the man next to me. He was Portuguese, living in a place I had never heard of: the islands of Archipelago Dos Bijagós, part of Guinea-Bissau in Africa. It sounds exotic and apparently is a prime spot for people who like to go fishing. The guy said, "If you have ever dreamed of catching giant fish from the sea, Bijagos might be your place!" He ran a guesthouse there, and told me a few tales of the kinds of people (mainly French) who go all the way there to find an unexplored, non-touristy destination.

As our conversation continued with details as rich as a novel, I spotted a senior couple secretly listening to our conversation. I looked intently at their timid expressions and I knew they wanted to say something. I gave them the opportunity by including pauses in our dreamy conversation, but they still did not join in or make any kind of attempt. So, I looked straight into the green eyes of the tall, athletic, sixty-something man and said, "You look like someone who would enjoy a fishing holiday!"

Puzzled, he looked at me, searching for words while hiding his embarrassment for having followed our talk. "Sorry," he said. "I mean, yes, I did a lot of fishing in Canada. I deeply enjoying fly fishing, but…"

Then he went on, telling a few stories of what clearly came across as his passion. He and his wife were English; they were retired and traveled for at least six months every year. They ended up exchanging details with the man for a possible trip to the island. The man later thanked me for bringing him into the conversation and admitted his reservations about intruding.

I asked, "Can you promise that you will take the opportunity to speak out next time something might pass you by?" He nodded with a big grin in his face. He understood that unless he overcomes some cultural and social barriers, he will never get what he wants. Besides, there is a tendency to give up, as enthusiasm fades with more ease when you get older. So it is crucial to practice flexibility and yes's.

Seniors must often take extra care in the planning, especially regarding healthcare. Be sensible when you decide on your destination. Get good health insurance and find out well in advance where your closest health facility will be once you are there. Try not to be too limiting, because there are hospitals everywhere; yes, they may have different standards, but getting an air ambulance flight elsewhere (not necessarily to your place of origin) can be easily arranged in an emergency with good travel insurance.

If you have physical challenges, be careful to not put yourself at risk by engaging in wild activities. For instance, if trekking could be taxing on your body, maybe you should put it off altogether. Otherwise, try to assess your body first and talk to people of your age group. Hire a porter if you want to do that, or join a fitness program. Make adjustments and go, if that's what you want to do, but do be prepared. A woman in her late-seventies climbed Mount Everest, so no excuses here! With a little extra planning, you will get to experience traveling safely.

Tip: *Find people of a similar age group who have successfully done what you are trying to do, so you can then ask them for their suggestions.*

Learning the language of the locals can be particularly difficult for this age group. If you find this to be true for you, it may be more practical to find a better way of communicating-- perhaps with body language. There are plenty of books on the subject. You simply need to practice a good attitude: smiling, using your hands, patience, and a great sense of observation. The Internet makes every phrasebook always handy; even mobile phones have applications that instantaneously translate words for you.

Activities depend on your level of fitness and stamina. Generally speaking, this group might enjoy the more cultural types of entertainment, as well as reading and spending more nights indoors.

In this Chapter, I have spoken about just three possibilities of what your traveling style could look like. I could further categorize other groups using different criteria than those presented here, but instead I encourage you to pick things of each style and mix them together. Especially if you are a total beginner, it is useful to get an idea regarding styles, as this will help you with other decisions such as your destination, when to go, or whether to go at all.

It is, however, not essential for you to plan so carefully, especially if you are free-spirited and like to leave a lot to fate. There are people who learn like this. Even when some misfortune happens to them, they react quickly and let the event enrich their traveling experience. On the opposite side of the spectrum, there are those who are meticulous in their organizing and will not change their traveling style. These fixated types, taken to the extreme, will benefit by viewing immobility as their perfect kind of trip!

Don't worry if you lack a definite style; this chapter has dealt with very approximate generalizations to simply give you a rough idea. You will be able to move on in your planning by reading the next chapter.

How and Where to Start.
How to Plan and Have Fun doing it

You might already have a possible destination, budget, and time frame planned by now. This chapter will help you to clarify it and to begin working on it. Before digging in, have a look at the most common mistakes and assumptions potential nomads make when beginning to plan.

Trouble spots

Cheap tickets

Statistics do vary in terms of when it is best to purchase international air tickets. So, it is a time-consuming practice rather than a time-sensitive one. Try **www.kayak.com** , **www.momondo.com** , **www.skyscanner.net**, or, if you are experienced in bargaining with local travel agencies, try **http://matrix.itasoftware.com** , as it lists only current airline offers-- it does not sell tickets.

Relying on travel guides

Inaccuracy issues are a constant even in the most reputable travelers' companions, such as Lonely Planet, Guide Routard, or the Rough Guide series. You are a nomad-- ask people instead of always looking in your guide!

Passport issues

Although your passport has an expiration date, it is good a practice to renew it six months before it expires, as many countries don't allow you in otherwise. Also, always check visa regulations and eligibility carefully.

Itinerary cancellations

Weather, strikes, political upheaval, missed connections, and so forth. --when plans must change, don't give up immediately. Do some research and always try to make your priority heard; sometimes canceling a destination is not necessary.

Maps

Some smartphones and tablets can use maps and nacvigation abilities with GPS-only settings, so you do not need a wifi hotspot to function. However not all apps have this offline option. The one I use is the free version of *Navigator.* Before you go, download the map of the country you are visiting when you are on wifi. Then later you can access it with the GPS-only function. It works!

Papers and stuff

Do not carry unnecessary paper, documents, photos, or anything else that can be deposited in the cloud. Yes, even reservations, and so forth. Get a free account at **www.mediafire.com** and one at **www.dropbox.com** .

Hiking gear

If you intend to do a lot of hiking, you might want to purchase special gear at home. In developing countries, if the equipment is available at all it will cost a fortune--even to rent it.

Pack light

I know that your luggage is your home. But really, you don't need much, and the weight you carry will stress you out. Everyone who has an overload will reach a point of near exhaustion and end up sending stuff back or donating it to others to lighten up.

How Long?

If this is one of your first trips, there is a good chance you will have to go back home at some point, as you will not be a full-time nomad yet. If you are a little older, you might feel financially secure enough to go on the road for good. You already know by now that my suggestion is to do it gradually. There are many possible reasons for some adjustment problems along the way, including:

- Inexperience
- Bad planning
- Bad company
- Personality clashes
- Cultural differences
- Lack of standards
- Acquiring/Letting go of habits
- Blindness to danger/opportunity

- Inappropriate behavior
- Holding on to old ways
- Commitments

As you continue reading this book, you will see both what can happen on the road and how to make sure a trip back home is handled with care. For now, just try to get an idea of a time frame; you will adjust it as you read, especially after Chapters 6 and 7.

When you plan for your first trip, you might be tempted to go "full-time nomad" without a return plan on the horizon. In your mind, this indefinite extension makes perfect sense. The problem is, it cannot be foretold how you're going to react to the new lifestyle. In a few months, the memories of your old life might make you start missing it—you might develop nostalgia for familiar people and places. In my experience, it won't hurt to have a "Plan B" involving going back. This might entail making sure you will have a roof over your head when you return, or even a job. Unless you swap your current home for an RV, in which case going home is only a matter of parking!

Ask yourself some questions. For example, if you sold all your belongings, would it be difficult for you to acquire them again? I personally cannot judge whether or not you should engage in being a full-time nomad. The point I am making is that with a little extra planning, you will have more options open to you as things change. One option, going part-time and then returning home, is what I see people doing, including me.

Psychologically, the part-time nomad walks around with more confidence, despite the many things that could cut a trip short. Preparing for them in advance helps to minimize this risk.

This is all you need to know at this stage in regards to choosing a time frame, since everyone is different. You won't find a definite answer in a book or travel guide; it is the road that will be your ultimate test and teacher.

Flow, or the lack thereof, could determine how long you are going to enjoy being a nomad. The people you meet can either inspire you or drag you down the wrong path. This is why deciding on a time frame can facilitate a more grounded approach to traveling, as opposed to a carefree, indefinite style. The price you pay is often just a little loss in adventure and a compromise with any free-spirited ideals you might have.

Money and Finances

Regarding budget, you should keep an eye on your spending. This is not a vacation where you can offset being a careless spender. You have to divide your current money to make it fit your time frame. It helps to know if you are in a position to earn an income on-site or remotely while away, or if you must rely on finding a job or putting in some hours of casual work if you need money.

There is a chance that a job might never be found. I've seen it far too many times, when people who are not well organized, make work a "mañana" priority, a Spanish attitude meaning "I'll do it tomorrow"—in other words, tomorrow never comes. So again, have a plan.

You could organize your financial plan like this:

Money
1) My savings

2) My budget

3) Money earned/ job

Your savings, for instance might be used in part to set your budget, a percentage of your budget might include money you will be earning while on the road.

Lay down some goals and rules, and check your progress daily. If you cannot stick to the plan, change it, or say to yourself, "I need to work harder next week".

Decide what you're going to do if you are looking for a job. Have an actions list!

Achieving anything in life takes work, and a nomadic lifestyle requires some action-driven behavior. This is common sense, but people tend to hate having to read it in a book. So, if you find yourself saying, "I already know that!" then ask yourself: why are you not actively doing it? Stop just dreaming and act, even if you must take baby steps before you can walk.

Some people have decided that they are bad with numbers, and others believe you need to be an organized person to be good with finances. These are just the most common excuses for avoiding the issue of budgeting or taking control of finances and money in general. Instead, what is true is that everyone can learn and apply a strategy effectively and to put themselves in control.

Tip: *If money saving is a problem, remember your "why" on a daily basis. Keep a separate bank account and make weekly deposits into it. Have another for emergencies. Write down five ways you can cut unnecessary expenditures or save money starting today.*

Being away for a long time requires the skill of money management, so start with that skill and it's a simple enough process to master. Do not let the lack of funding delay or stop you from pursuing your trip. When facing difficulties, visualize your trip for five minutes daily. Just have fun closing your eyes and imagining that you are there. This will create more desire and will also stimulate the mind to come up with a solution. "The way will suddenly appear," the Magician would say.

Create an Inventory

I would like to draw your attention to a very important aspect of planning: building an inventory. The following method is the most useful, and deciding to do it will prepare you psychologically for your upcoming trip. It might even speed you up, making you ready sooner than your priorly envisioned departure date.

You need to create an inventory of whatever you have, all your possessions, and clear the clutter once and for all. Getting rid of stuff is therapeutic (I will explain why later), and should not stop or be limited to getting rid of only clothes. Most of us have done that, and doesn't it feel good when you do it?

An Asian-heritage technique called *Feng- Shui*[4] explains how clearing clutter has life-changing potential[5]. Turning the acton of getting rid of clutter into artform *Feng Shui* insists that mastering the process is a life- changing experience! (The Magician agrees!). There is a book I suggest you to read, a classic in this topic: *"Clear Your Clutter With Feng-Shui"* by Karen Kingston.

The author suggests the following process:
Start by selecting your unwanted clothes, and give them to people or to charity. If you really want to use them to make cash, try selling them on eBay. However, this is time-consuming; it might be better to organize a garage sale.

Now, what if I ask you to do it again? The first time, you threw away only what was long overdue to go. The second time, apply more stringent criteria. For example, this time apply the "haven't worn for more than a year" criteria for clothes that have to go.

Do not use the excuse "I'll lose weight tomorrow" as a reason to keep the skirt you struggle to zip. If it doesn't fit, throw it away. "No, but... You don't

---

4   A Chinese system for positioning a building and the objects within a building in a way that is thought to agree with spiritual forces and to bring health and prosperity
(http://www.merriam-webster.com/dictionary/feng%20shui)

5 Clutter is low, stagnant, blocked energy that drains energy from you and lowers the quality of your life.
(http://fengshui.about.com/od/clearyourcluttertips/ss/feng-shui-clutter-clearing-system-prepare.htm)

understand, it is still new!" Forget those remarks too; it has to go if you haven't worn it for a while. Frankly, it is no longer your size, so why keep it in your closet?

Think how happy it will make someone who finds a brand-new skirt in a thrift store or charity shop!

Things to throw away:
- Worn out
- Broken and irreparable (e.g., appliances, toys)
- Dated
- Damaged
- Not in use

Things to sell:
- Collectibles, antiques (do you really enjoy having them?)
- Branded
- Usable by others
- High monetary value

If something is of sentimental value, consider taking a picture for a scrapbook, or keeping a portion of it as memorabilia.

There are some exceptions. If you can use clothing as material for another garment or project, keep it. If it is something you love to wear for rare special occasions, keep it. If formal wear, a tuxedo or bridesmaid's dress, can be used for a future costume party, then you keep those.

This procedure will kick in a psychological chain reaction regarding how you treat attachments. The process also creates space for new things to come. Stop! The Magician whould have liked to give you this pearl of wisdom!

Here is a great Pinterest page for more ideas:

http://www.pinterest.com/source/smead.com

Consider going in each room of your house and making a list of things that can be eliminated. Then next to each room write a date by which the room must be cleared. From that list, pick up ten things you can give away this week.

List five situations, people, or commitments you will be better off without and, if feasible, start to work them out of your life by ending them gradually. Yes, clearing clutter is also intended for relationships that are no longer serving you or are stagnant, lifeless.

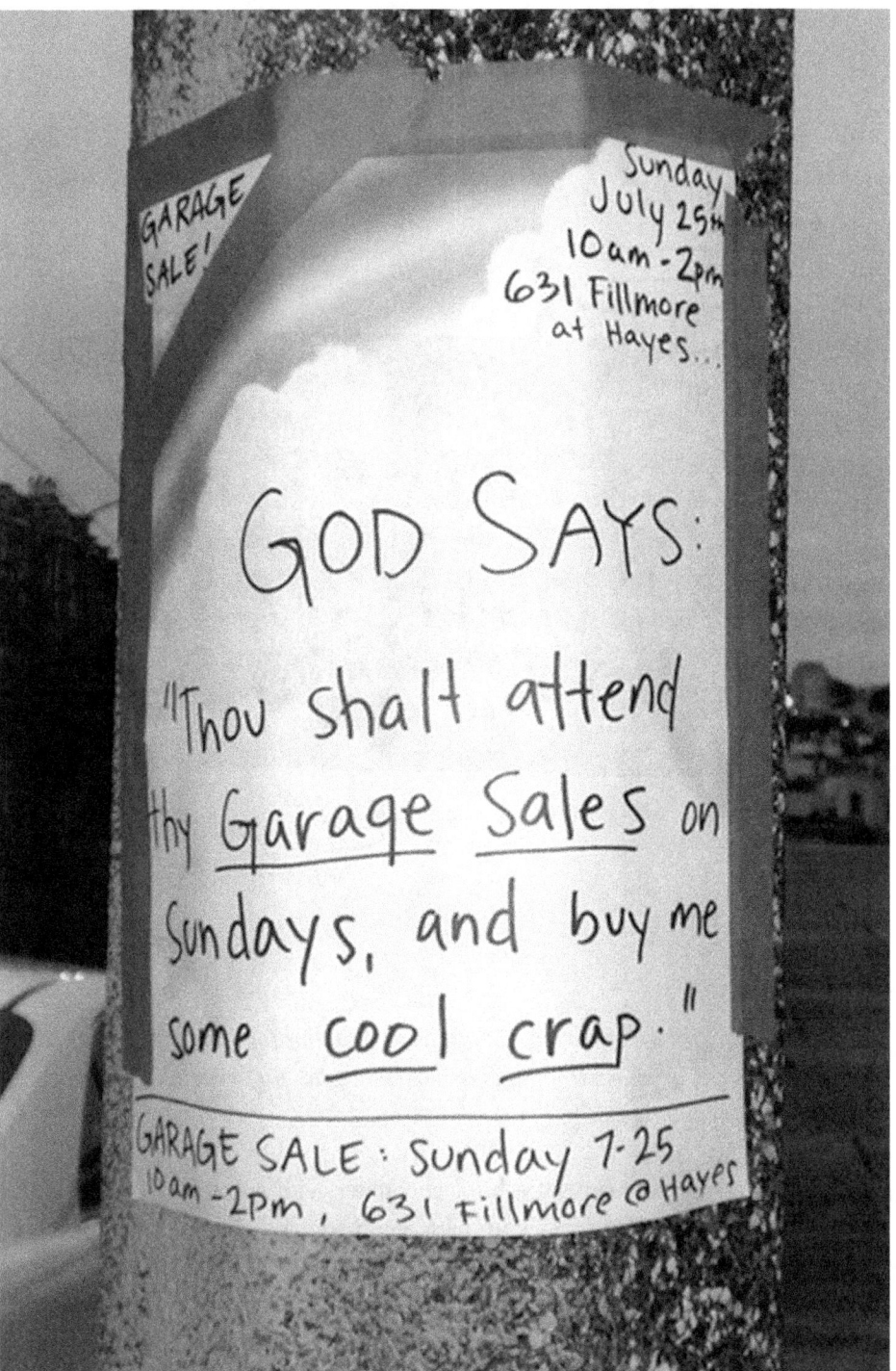

Magician likes to add:

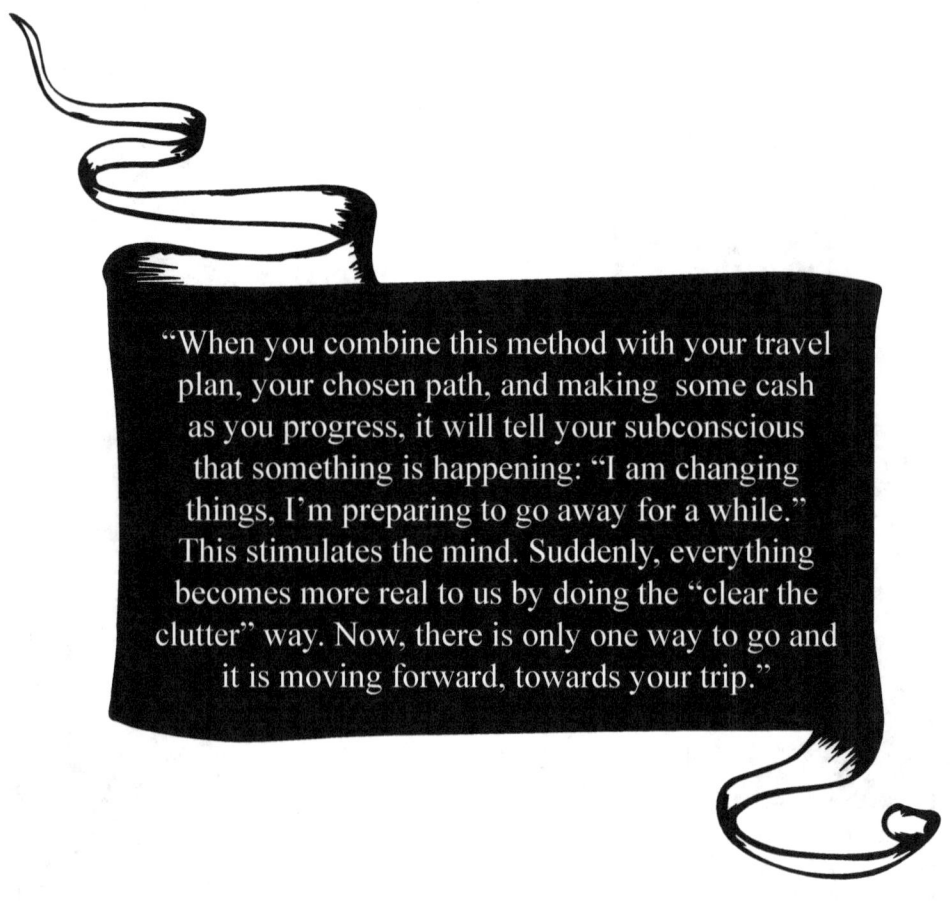

"When you combine this method with your travel plan, your chosen path, and making some cash as you progress, it will tell your subconscious that something is happening: "I am changing things, I'm preparing to go away for a while." This stimulates the mind. Suddenly, everything becomes more real to us by doing the "clear the clutter" way. Now, there is only one way to go and it is moving forward, towards your trip."

Tip: *When you are clearing out clutter, watch out for things to give away to friends. Thinking of your belongings as possible gifts for someone else is a very useful mindset while traveling.*

Sometimes, the intensity of a brief encounter with someone you will never meet again, or who might cross your path again someday, will demand a sort of recognition from you. Get used to giving your belongings away to them, just to symbolize the importance of the wonderful time you had together. These moments of connection are just simply magical. It's okay, I can say that; the Magician is sleeping now.

Chose a Destination

Destinations, of course, are many. The list on the next page will give you some ideas. You are free to add your favorite spot if I did not mention it. Consider it a shortlist from a vast array of choices in this big planet, waiting to be explored by people like you and me. These suggestions might evoke curiosity (by now you know my style on what I like you to do). If you feel captivated by them, do further research on the Internet--look in forums, or at pictures and videos to get a sense of what they might be like. I have given them some kind of category, nothing is stopping you putting that category into Google and ask the search engine something like, "best romantic places in the world." See what you get. Be creative.

Inexpensive Destinations

- *Asia (except Japan, and Singapore or anywhere where permits are expensive, i.e. Brunei)*
- *Africa (except safari destinations)*
- *Portugal*
- *Nicaragua*
- *Mexico*
- *Guatemala*
- *Peru*
- *Ecuador*
- *Bolivia*
- *Colombia*
- *Chile*
- *Paraguay*
- *Uruguay*

Grand Adventures

- *Tour the Sahara on a camel*
- *Climb Kilimanjaro*
- *Go cycling in India*
- *Explore New Zealand*
- *Go on safari in Zambia*
- *Hike the Inca trail in Peru*

Other Adventurous Destinations

- *Mauritania*
- *Ethiopia*
- *Indonesia*
- *Amazon jungle*
- *Iran*
- *The Alps*
- *Jordan*
- *Nepal*
- *Rwanda*
- *Antarctica & Cape Horn*

Expensive Destinations
- *USA*
- *Europe*
- *Australia*
- *Antarctica*
- *Brazil*
- *Panama*
- *Belize*
- *Venezuela*
- *Argentina*

Good for the Soul
- *Tibet*
- *India*
- *Bali*
- *Alto Paraiso, Brazil*
- *Ibiza, Spain*
- *The Amazon Basin (Brazil/Peru/Ecuador)*
- *Sedona, California, USA*
- *Byron Bay, Australia*
- *Luxor, Egypt*
- *Niagara Falls, New York, USA*
- *Victoria Falls, Zimbabwe*
- *Grand Canyon, Arizona, USA*
- *Big Sur, California, USA*
- *Glastonbury, England*
- *Sintra, Portugal*

Perfect for Artists
- *Costa Rica*
- *Western Australia*
- *Santa Fe, New Mexico, USA*
- *Bali, Indonesia*
- *Laos*
- *Luxor, Egypt*
- *Cinque Terre, Italy*
- *Deia, Spain*
- *Oia, Greece*

- *Lake District, England*
- *Umbria, Italy*
- *Cadaques, Spain*
- *Cuba*
- *San Cristobal, Mexico*
- *Berlin, Germany*
- *New Orleans, Louisiana, USA*
- *Venice, Italy*

Exotic & Extraordinary

- *Republic of Seychelles*
- *Kyoto, Japan*
- *Fiji*
- *French Polynesia*
- *Madagascar*
- *El Nido, Philippines*
- *Republic of the Maldives*
- *Filicudi, Italy*
- *Nookta Island, Canada*
- *Alaska, USA*
- *Torres del Paine, Chile*
- *Iceland*
- *Lencois sand dunes, Maranhão, Brazil*
- *Angkor Wat, Cambodia*
- *Tekal, Guatemala*
- *Uluru National Park, Australia*
- *Cappadocia, Turkey*
- *The Fjords, Norway*
- *Antarctica*
- *The Great Wall, China*
- *The Sahara, Morocco, Mauritania*
- *Galapagos, Ecuador*

Off the Beaten Path

- *Raja Ampat, West Papua, Indonesia*
- *Marquesas Islands, French Polynesia*
- *Nosy Be Island, Madagascar*
- *Bijagos Islands, Guinea-Bissau*

- *Republic of Mozambique*
- *Perhentian Islands, Malaysia*
- *Easter Island, Polynesia*
- *Virgin Islands*
- *Myanmar*
- *Bhutan*
- *Koh Rong, Cambodia*

Glamorous Destinations

- *Gstaad, Switzerland*
- *Miami, Florida, USA*
- *Telluride and Aspen, Colorado, USA*
- *The Hamptons, New York, USA*
- *Ibiza, Spain*
- *Cote D'Azur, France*
- *St Bart, France (yes, St Bart is still French, although in the Caribbean!)*
- *Trancoso, Brazil*
- *Punta del 'Este, Uruguay*
- *Mykonos, Greece*
- *Capri, Porto Cervo, Italy*
- *Dubai, United Arab Emirates*

Plan for Alternate Destinations

Never plan for only one destination; have a few in mind. If one destination is not what you thought it would be, you can move on to the next. Your experiences gained while traveling will help you to gather information about possible future destinations. But, when you are just beginning, ask people who have been there, leverage travelers' forums on the Internet, or read this guide or another travel book about the places you want to go.

Once, I was in Australia and hadn't engaged in much planning for my trip. The next stop was going to be New Zealand, a country I knew very little about. I had decided to go there because I had a couple of good Kiwi friends in London who I considered to be very nice people, and because I had been told the scenery and ecosystem were among the most beautiful in the world. This might well have been true… But I never made it there after all. I canceled my plane ticket, because I was not so sure about New Zealand and decided to change my destination.

From my traveler's dream bucket list, I knew that I had always wanted to see French Polynesia. The change was not simple: I would have to purchase a brand-new ticket and work out a four-week itinerary in five days. What tipped the scale for me was noticing by chance a picture in my Sydney hotel room. It was hanging in a strange place, completely hidden behind my bed. I took it out and saw a photo of Moorea, a famous Polynesian island. I took it as a sign: I had to go!

Now, if I had planned my trip to New Zealand by gathering extra information and stories ahead of time, I would have had a clear plan and Moorea would have felt less tempting. Not knowing much about New Zealand did not ignite a strong desire for it as a possible destination.

Moorea, on the other hand, was right up my alley. It was a dream destination, as was Bora Bora in the same archipelago. They had been dream destinations for me for a long time. I was always eager to listen to people who had been there; they told me many things that made planning an itinerary seem easy. They made loose suggestions about prices (advising me that it was going to be really expensive), and gave clues about the local people as well as their customs and fascinating history. I had pictured breathtaking tropical scenery of turquoise oceans, deep green jungles, and majestic mountain tops to climb.

Of course, I could have rescheduled New Zealand into one of my future trips, although this would apply to Polynesia too. I tell this story to show that because I did not plan well, I faced the consequences of making quick changes.

The trip in Polynesia suffered because it relied too much on credit cards. I had a fair number of good times, but also bad ones: there was always something not flowing. Though I encountered difficulties because some of the advice I received was inaccurate, the beauty of the country made up for it. The journey ended up being a tough one for a combination of reasons: choosing unpleasant hotels, failing to communicate with insular locals, facing the constant exploitation of indigenous culture, as well as picking destinations that lacked opportunities to meet other adventure-seeking nomads.

This was the price I paid for rushing out on a poorly made itinerary. I could have had an unforgettable time if perhaps I had given it more thought and spent longer in the planning stage.

Since this accident, I have not changed plans in my travel so drastically, and I plan well with each trip. What I like to do is to always have an itinerary planned for several possible destinations; if I don't like one, I move on. This is easier done when traveling alone, although it can be done with your traveling companion too. When I have a companion, I value him or her and make a point of being flexible. So, if someone wants to stay and the other wants to move on, it's a temporary goodbye instead of making someone suffer by going to a place where they don't want to go. Plan for this too, if you have a companion, by asking about their degree of flexibility.

While on the subject, even this trip taught be that destinations have to remain flexible so we can flow better. I remember leaving Papeete airport at the very end of my trip, it was then that I met a fellow nomad. He had a huge grin lighting his face and was wearing Polynesian leys and garlands as colorful ornaments. Rather than being dropped from a luxury resort (as you could expect from the way he was dressed), he had just lived a special experience. He told me that on his first night there he casually met some locals who took care of him by inviting him to stay at their house. Later then, thanks to their extended family connections, they helped him through his itinerary, which was flexible enough to accommodate new destinations. He was treated like family and had an awesome time.

I would have loved to be feeling as positive as he did, but I was not. However, meeting him confirmed to me that it was not the country or its people, but rather my own approach to the whole trip that failed somehow.

Let's assume you might have chosen a country to explore, read the guide, and spoken to people. You have hand-picked a few destinations as a result. As you are planning possible itineraries, you then will have to decide on how long you want to stay in each place. Personally, the most appealing way to travel for me is to find a place I like and stop there for a while, even if it means sacrificing other places that are in the itinerary. How long is a while? You can define it or leave it open, taking into consideration the overall duration of the whole trip. For me, if I really resonate with a place I encounter, and it ticks many of my criteria for awesomeness, I like my "visa" to say undefined, if you know what I mean…

The nomad I met in Polynesia did just that-he changed his itinerary with confidence as he put his trust in his hosts. He kept evaluating his itinerary as he progressed with the trip, keeping the time frame flexible.

Your style, however, might be different. Decide on your flexibility in advance, especially if you have a partner or companion. If you find the answers in advance then you won't fall for a place just because "it just seems nice." You will have a more grounded approach meeting your desires and needs.

Reflect on the following:

- Are you in search of a place you would like to live and work in for a while?
- What really stands out as important to you?
- What is your criteria for recognizing the right place? For instance:
  o Does this place have nightlife or not?

  o Is it very peaceful / buzzy?

- o   Is it cosmopolitan?
- o   Do expats live there?
- o   How important is money there?
- o   Are people's attitudes welcoming?
- o   How is the political climate?

You will still have doubts, and no destination is perfect. But that shouldn't stop you from exploring your options and deciding if a place is right for you, whether it will make you truly satisfied or not. Once you define what you want, you will know very quickly if a particular place is what you are looking for. It might take some time if you are a novice traveler to know what you want.

Magician disagrees:

"Deciding which places are right for you is part of the self-discovery journey. Being a nomad gives you the freedom to pack your bags and go when the time is right."

I hope what I have said so far about planning will motivate you to get a journal and an organizer, as they will be helpful in putting a plan together.

Planning Checklist

Now that you have read this chapter, put it to use as soon as possible. Here is a checklist to help you:

- Make sure to inform your loved ones of your plan
- Organize your finances, utility bills, service contracts, and bank accounts-you don't want to find yourself in deep debts or without electricity when you return.
- Organize your belongings
- De-clutter every aspect of your life
- Decide what type of destination you would like to explore
- Choose a few destinations
- Make criteria to help you decide how interested you are in each destination and how long you would like to stay (if you plan to move permanently, check out this website for valuable tips on moving abroad, and integrate them into your plan: **http://www.theexpathub.com/emigration-checklist**)
- Keep yourself on track by setting milestones and deadlines, creating an action list between now and your planned departure date.
- Have a "Plan B", including how to get home on short notice.
- Make changes as you progress.

All I have discussed will help you to avoid getting caught setting unrealistic expectations. If your dream ends up not what you have forecasted, planning ahead will ensure that you have enough resources to adjust to reality with ease.

Now are you all ready to go? Not yet! First, let's decide if it makes sense to earn money during your trip, and if so, how you will do it.

Earning Money While Traveling

"A business that makes nothing but money is a poor business."
Henry Ford

Yes, I'm Working

"If the world is an oyster, you are never going to find the pearl unless you learn to live in it. Find work to do and before you know it, the precious jewel will be standing right in front of you."

In this chapter, we will explore a very interesting concept: making your trip profitable. This works differently than how most of us are accustomed to. The whole idea of working might be a daunting thought for some, especially to those who have never enjoyed it. In what follows, I promise to reinvent this by making work a fun activity.

Have you noticed that many millionaires still work? They do so by choice, not because they have to; they work because they enjoy it. Work can be fun, it is just a matter of finding out how you can plan for this and learning new skills or turning your current ones into cash.

Consider the digital age we are in, with its countless new, untapped opportunities that fit well with the mobile lifestyle. A nomad can often work regardless of location. This new scenarios of working in the twenty-first century can help nomads accumulate wealth more quickly, taking advantages of riding the workplace's trends. The hippie-idealist traveler might need to embrace a lifestyle in which any idea has a cash equivalent potential and can be traded with ease, facilitating a prosperous outlook. The yuppie-hipster nomad, in turn, might have to reconcile consumer priorities with a Spartan, carefree lifestyle. Such new breeds of nomads, far from being perceived as social dropouts, will be seen as trailblazers, people to emulate to find success.

If money flows, then you need to seriously ask yourself how you would like to use it: would you rather travel and experience sleeping in a hammock, or would you prefer to rent a plush pad as a temporary home? I ask you to consider what gems can be found in a night where you'll be at one with nature, swinging under a roofless sky, listening to the sound of the ocean crashing to shore. Will that experience justify missing out on guilty pleasures and an extravagant lifestyle? Sincerely, this is a predicament I am happy to live with.

If money is a problem for you, instead, you will have no choice and you must decide how you will earn it while traveling.

I will tell you a story. I was in Mykonos, one of the most beautiful and glamorous Greek Islands. I had just finished a degree in Anthropology; as a treat, I decided to be there the entire season, from May to November.

I had budgeted well and I had plenty of savings, so working was not on my list of things to do. I had not even considered it. I had worked hard for my degree and I wanted a bit of fun and rest --certainly not work!

Things changed when I saw that my newfound friends on the island were all working—even a couple of celebrities were doing something. Thomas, a Swedish barman, made me realize that I would be spending most of my savings, if not all, without a job. Also, I would eventually get bored! He convinced me to look for a job.

It took me only two days before I found a job working as a waiter in a restaurant for just a few hours in the evenings. The work was not hard and it turned out to be a lot of fun. It was not the type of job I would ever have considered in London, but for Mykonos it was ideal.

Working there brought me closer to the local life, and deciding to live on my wages instead of my savings also put a limit on my hedonistic side. I could have kept on bingeing and partying through the entire season. Instead, working made me feel useful and I enjoyed the island even more. I truly felt enriched by the whole experience.

With the money I made, I kept traveling for another year and even visited some regular customers from the restaurant.

I tell this story because at first, judging by the money I had, there was no indication that I needed any form of earnings. Contrary to the belief I held before, I discovered how working can be enjoyable and that it can breaks the monotony you will eventually come across. Mykonos, for instance, is a small island. Yes, it has nice beaches and a good nightlife, which can be fun for a few weeks, but not months.

When you work only to pay the bills or to make progress with your career, it can be a very stressful routine. While traveling, you can commit to a job with a different attitude. Looking back, serving tables made me more flexible. There are so many jobs that you can do; if you consider them part of using your time profitably, working can be rewarding and fun.

As a nomad building up your traveling experiences, you will soon note an improved capacity to mix with the local culture. This fact automatically brings forward more opportunities and getting a job will seem easy; working in a local business is usually a wonderful experience.

Seasonal Jobs

Even if you don't like them, do consider spending a season in a very touristy, cosmopolitan, well-known destination. It will be easier to find work there, and the variety of people will open up new perspectives and help you to look at life with different eyes. If you are single or divorced, be warned that those places have a reputation for being frequented by Cupid!

I have had the pleasure of meeting countless people who first met in heavily exploited, "tourist Mecca" and are now happily married. The advantage of meeting someone while traveling is that you might already share a passion for traveling. Having a nomadic heart in common can mean a lot in a relationship.

The wisdom of the Magician:

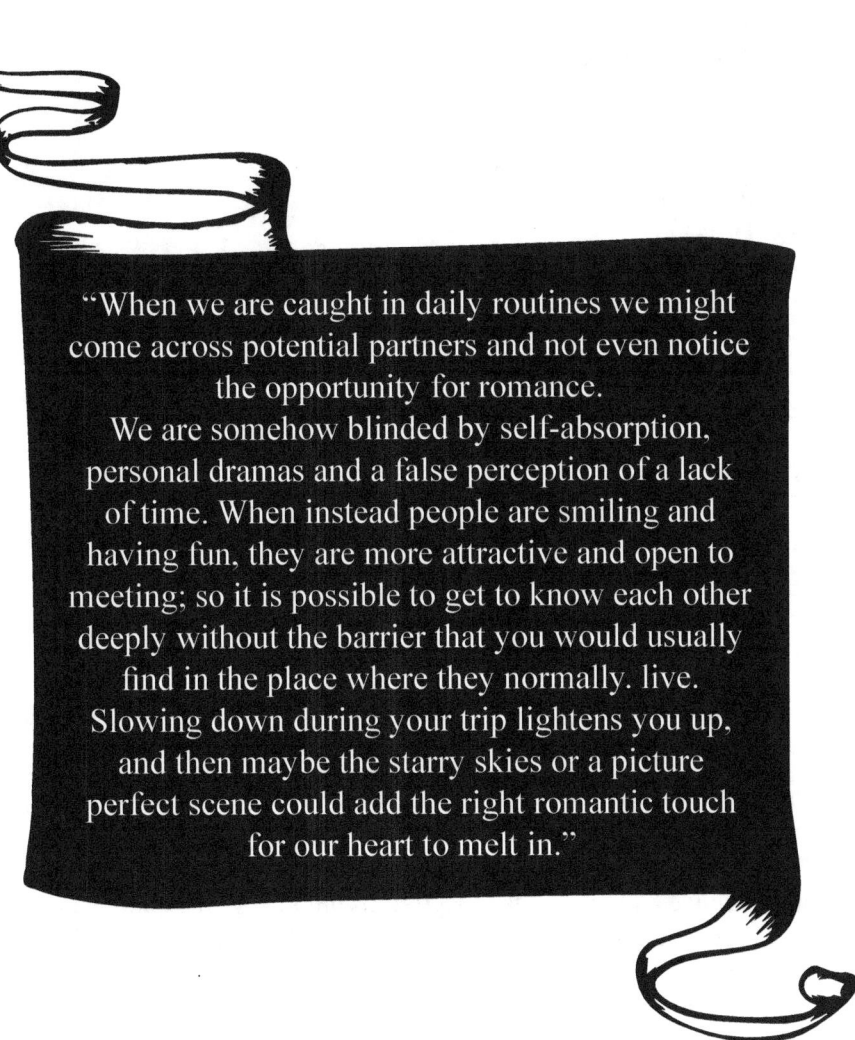

"When we are caught in daily routines we might come across potential partners and not even notice the opportunity for romance. We are somehow blinded by self-absorption, personal dramas and a false perception of a lack of time. When instead people are smiling and having fun, they are more attractive and open to meeting; so it is possible to get to know each other deeply without the barrier that you would usually find in the place where they normally. live. Slowing down during your trip lightens you up, and then maybe the starry skies or a picture perfect scene could add the right romantic touch for our heart to melt in."

Hey, Magician! That sure is romantic, but I must get back on topic. Do you mind?

Okay, work can also be a good way to find out what you like to do. Here is a list of the most common jobs offered in touristy destinations:
- Tour operator
- Travel guide
- Teacher
- Hotel staff
- Restaurant/bar/club staff
- Promoter
- Driver
- Realtor or time-share representative
- Cleaner
- Baby sitter
- Travel agency staff
- Car hire staff
- Beach club staff
- Scuba instructor
- Sports instructor/coach
- Entertainer
- Security officer
- Spa staff
- Sports center staff
- Amusement park staff

These are just a few examples of a very long list. Forget the "previous experience" normally asked for at home. In these areas, plenty of non-experienced people will get hired just by showing their will to work.

While it is a valuable asset, you often don't even need to show a resume. A positive attitude and foreign language skills are in absolute demand, and learning a few words in a number of different languages beforehand is totally achievable. This will impress your employer and the tourists will love you for it.

Look at the list that I made and try to imagine what you can have fun doing. Remember that you are not going to commit to it for a lifetime to it--only a few short months. Just make sure it leaves enough free-time for you; I have seen many people who ended up working all the time. It does not have to be like that; shop around. Sometimes people feel they are too old to do seasonal work. This is not true; active seniors can handle the hours of work too! Many work even after retirement, so no excuses there. You will find something to do.

What About Freelance?

It is quite "old school" to get a seasonal job; these days there is also the possibility of working freelance, often just using a laptop.

While the majority of nomads still rely on scouting for, or being offered, more traditional jobs, improvements in digital connections brought forward an increasing trend in digital nomads who can freelance as their primary form of earning an income.

To build a freelance business, you must explore the more entrepreneurial aspects of you. Some will resist the idea, saying, "No, I am not an entrepreneur!" I would invite you to rethink that

Find your professional passion

It is well known that amongst entrepreneurs who succeed are the ones with with a strong passion. If you don't know what your passion is, help is on hand. In the appendix, you will find an exercise you can do to get an idea of how to find your passions. While it is not perfect, it is a beginner's exercise that opens the door to look inwards.

Life-coaching is an industry dedicated to solving this type of self-enquiry. Consider, perhaps, working closely with a coach. Finding the things you are passionate about and figuring out how to tap into them can be solved in a single coaching session--or it can take up to six, it really depends.

It takes time to clarify your passions, even with the help of a coach. What most people will end up with is just a blueprint, meant to be explored day-by-day. By progressively asking the right questions over some time, you can view all of your past as well as your present with a new awareness. Keep a journal in which you can write your daily insights, as it will help you to integrate your learning.

Tip: *Imagine a passionate life! Spend five minutes every day imagining yourself feeling awake and alive in all activities that you do. As you repeat this, the images of that life will get stronger and you will behave differently.*

Once you have found what you are passionate about--either through the suggested appendix exercise, coaching sessions, or your own imagination--choose three passions that might be turned into a freelance job, business, or profession. For example, you are reading a book that has been born from putting a passion (in this case, traveling) into a workable creative venture.

As you gather ideas for these future professions, you will soon notice that some require skills you don't have. If you are really interested in that profession,

you will need to learn the skills. There are a number of ways of doing this:
- Trial and error
- Study: find someone to teach you, in a class or online
- Apprenticeship: find someone who is good at it and work six months for free in exchange for training
- A combination of these

Personally, I use Google and YouTube to find tutorials, researching what is available for free first. Use Google to search for sites and blogs with related information; use YouTube to find how-to videos from experts in the field.

If I cannot find what I need there, I go to sites like **www.Elance.com**, **www.Odesk.com** or **www.upwork.com** to see if an expert is willing to teach me over the net or if they know someone who will. Sometimes I can learn tricks of the trade by interviewing an expert; this way I can use their interview as a learning tool. Skype is a good way to do this, because you can easily record your Skype call using third-party software. Go to Skype Support at **www.skypesupport.com** to look up your operating system and find out which tools you can use.

Online freelance work

I prefer skills that can be learned online, and that I can offer remotely myself. The digital age has opened the possibility for you to offer your services wherever you are.

The sites mentioned earlier (Elance, Odesk and Upwork) are well-known platforms that companies use to find and hire freelancers. They are extremely safe for getting paid, because they collect the money beforehand from employers.

The funds can be delivered gradually, through milestones (if the job is delivered in stages) or on completion once the employer is satisfied.

The job terms do vary; they are discussed and negotiated before the job starts.

You will be competing with other freelancers who will bid on the same job offers. It can take a while to earn your reputation on these sites. Here is a link to videos that shows you how to speed up the process:

https://www.youtube.com/watch?v=8Sb6Bg-Ysy0
https://www.youtube.com/watch?v=huRP7qXc2u0

Here is a list of professionals who might teach you skills that you can offer remotely:

- Online marketing strategists/consultants
- IT managers/developers/programmers
- Database managers
- Bookkeepers/accountants/CPAs
- Lawyers
- Personal assistants
- Web designers
- Writers
- Editors
- Bloggers
- Podcasters
- Photographers & videographers
- Affiliate salespeople
- Social media managers
- Product reviewers/ beta testers
- Arbitrage Sellers: find bargains to resell for profit
- Online product & store managers
- Graphic designers
- Online professors
- Personal & professional coaches
- Consultants & advisors
- Online advertising campaign managers
- Customer support
- Agents (travel, insurance, etc.)
- Investors/traders
- Transcriptionists
- Translators
- Researchers/information providers

Build an online business

If your passion moves you more towards a business idea, make it mobile. Nowadays stores are closing not simply because of an economic down turn or because of corporate competition. They are moving online, selling from a website; often the old-fashioned warehouse is gone and the product line is produced and fulfilled on demand.

Did you know that you can buy ready-made products with "white labels?" Meaning that they are ready to be branded by whoever chooses to buy them, as they have no proprietary licensing rights attached. The process is ridiculously easy. China is the biggest player in this marketplace, however the list extends to other countries too. A major online third-party database of suppliers can be found at: **www.Alibaba.com**, an eBay-style marketplace. It primarily lists Chinese wholesalers, although it also has worldwide inclusion. If selling physical goods is not your style, you can sell information in the forms of books, video, audio, or consultancy.

How to Start Working Now

Learn as you go

If you really cannot bear the time it takes to learn a new skill and want to start traveling immediately, then I suggest you adopt an "on the road approach."

While on the road, talk to as many people as possible who have figured out ways to earn money and offer to ease their load for a little while as an apprentice.

Sometimes by doing this you will earn money, sometimes a skill or favor. Be selective: a smart choice would be to identify and become a helper for someone who earns good money using skills you want to master.

If you have had camping experience, you probably know how to start a fire. You learned that skill from someone else because it was necessary to survive. A nomad must be able to adapt to new environments quickly, so learning workable skills is as vital as learning how to start a fire while camping. There are always people who are willing to teach you; just keep on being curious, interested, and adventurous.

Those are the attitudes that will make you go far. Be watchful of your resistance—the "I can't do that" conditioning. It will try to play with your psychology to inhibit you.

The Magician adds:

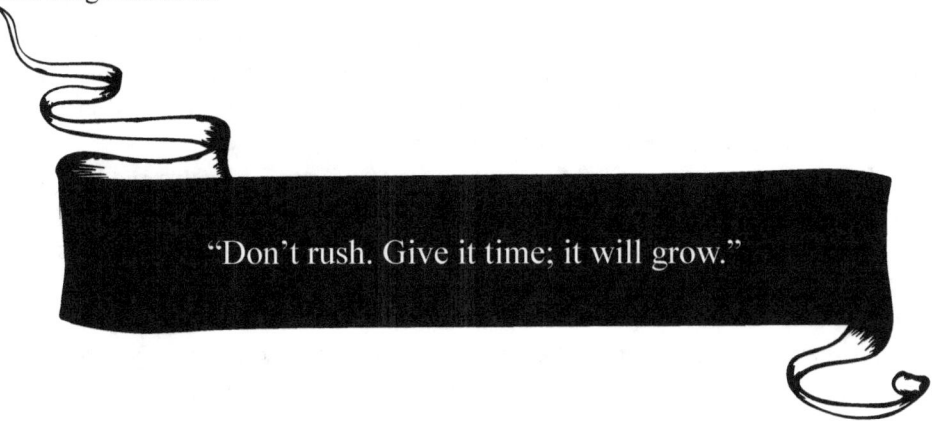

"Don't rush. Give it time; it will grow."

Even a seasoned nomad like me has to work to remember this. I was with a group of people and someone had a guitar. A girl wanted to teach me a very simple song on it. Although only few of us were there, initially I said "No, it is not for me, I can't play the guitar." She asked kindly if I would like to learn. The temptation at this point, I must admit, was to say, "No, it is all right," because I did not want to appear clumsy or hopeless when given the guitar.

But instead of giving in to this fear, I said, "Yes; I can't promise anything, but I will have a go." Because deep down, I knew how much I would love to learn to play guitar.

She was very patient and no one in the small group laughed at my mistakes. To learn the tune took rather a long time, I must say, but it was a little breakthrough for me. Now, whenever I meet someone with a guitar, I ask them to teach me a little. Who knows, one day I may teach others or even turn guitar playing into a fantastic traveling profession. Leveraging my online skills, I could even take the time and create a series of videos tutorials that I could sell for a profit.

Language skills

The nomad's number one skill is one you are born with: your mother tongue. If you are bilingual, you have even more to offer. Teaching a language locally or offering it as e-tutoring can add the easiest income on the planet. It won't make you rich, though, as there are many people doing it.

Think about investing in a good book about a sound teaching methodology you can put to use, or looking for online tutors who might help you. Some people instead simply stick to a more spontaneous way of teaching, or they just offer conversation lessons for more advanced levels.

Internet platforms you can use are Google Hangouts for groups and Skype for one-on-ones.

If you choose to go into e-tutoring, charge only a little money at first, as there is competition and there can be fierce competition in the jungle! You need positive feedback from digital users as well as testimonials on your blog. If you don't already have one, I suggest you begin a blog to let people know what you do. Also, take classes yourself from people who e-tutor, so as to experience it firsthand

More information about working while traveling

If you want more in-depth information about ways of earning while traveling, I am writing an entire book about it. If you are interested please register here:

www.goingnomadbook.com/upcoming

This way I will be ready to tell you when the book is being published. Registering your email entitles you for an exclusive offer--while you wait, you will receive a free Internet marketing training which is going to introduce you with selling online.

In the upcoming book, you will also find more advanced strategies to earning a mobile income, such as property investing and trading stocks. These are more traditional methods and in the past have dominated the travel-as-a-lifestyle scene.

Now, though, the people who make heaps of money are the ones who leverage the World Wide Web through online marketing. Often referred to as the "new gold rush," online marketing attracts many opportunities seekers because of how potentially profitable it is. Be careful! Scam artists are very skillful in selling courses with unrealistic promises. Failing prey to possible "get rich quick" schemes is extremely easy.

I created this training tutorial primarily to help you to stay away from scams. Online marketing is complex. If you have never done it, instead of struggling to find what works and possibly making costly mistakes, you could implement some of the guidelines included in the free step-by-step instructions.

Chapter 5

The New Life Begins

"You must live in the present, launch yourself on every wave, find your eternity in each moment."
Henry David Thoreau

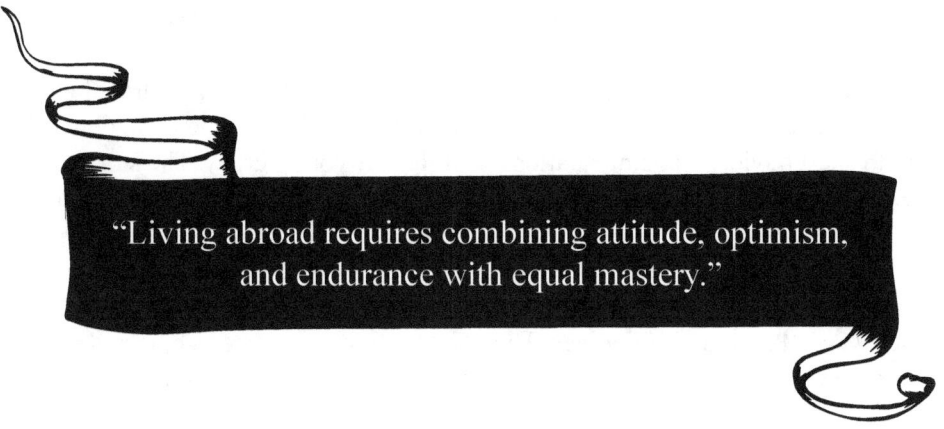

"Living abroad requires combining attitude, optimism, and endurance with equal mastery."

In this chapter, you will find the answer to what to do once your trip begins. It is possible that by now you have a date in mind and a list of destinations. What you need is clarification on what a destination can offer so you can evaluate it better. This chapter deals both with the travelers on their first short trip and with people who choose long-term destinations.

You might not know it where those destinations are, since I am sure many of you simply want to travel around a region freely. Let's start with those types of people first.

The Journey Begins

All those months spent dreaming and planning will build momentum towards the departure date. You will feel a mixture of excitement, fear, and building expectations for this potentially life-changing journey.

The problem is, despite all of the planning involved, it is unlikely that your trip will exactly fulfill your expectations. It is not a matter of accuracy in your planning stage, but rather that being on the road will always surprise you. This is not something negative, because most of the time it will motivate you to let go, embrace new perspectives, and experience flow. Treat the planning as a preparation to deal with whatever you might find rather than as a bible--a strict story in which everything is predetermined and written. Instead, it is more like an open book with blank pages to be filled in.

If this is your first trip, especially if you are on your own, the first thing traveling will teach you is how to open up while meeting strangers. You, as a priority, need to connect with other nomads. This is practical and adds fun to your journey.

The sooner you master it, the more successful you will be. Your travel will be smoother. Take everyone as a potential example of a living guidebook, delivering the freshest advice, recommendations, and tips for your journey. The stories these people tell will make you taste what it is to be a nomad and will ground you in the idea that now you too have joined this exclusive club.

Practically, you might want other nomads to join you in things such as organizing transportation. I faced this problem countless times. Amongst those, once was in Palawan, Philippines. The infrastructure of this tropical island is quite poor; it does not have many roads and the ones that are available are very bad even in a 4X4 at a cruising speed of 20mph. Going by boat was an option, but you could not always find scheduled services, and chartering a boat is expensive. In these situations, befriending some travelers with the same destination becomes vital, especially if your time is cut short by any other commitments. In Palawan, I got a hold of four people with the same destination but with different departure dates. I also persuaded another two to change their itinerary slightly to finally end up with seven people, just enough to make chartering the boat sensible.

What I have just described is extremely common, so take advantage by choosing accommodations where other travelers hang out or else find another setting where you might meet them. Travel together, have fun with them, and bond at every opportunity. While In Australia, America, or Europe, the hostels are where to find like-minded travelers. In Asia and Latin America, you can find them often just by picking a well-beaten path, a landmark, or a nomad's word-of-mouth secret place.

I often suggest overland trips for variety. Overland can include traveling with any form of transport on land excluding flying. You could organize this by charter and hiring private vehicles independently or by join overlanding tours. Expeditions are organized that cover the length of entire continents, aimed at people with different degrees of fitness and senses of adventure. People can choose to spend months or weeks; it is up to them to decide, as they can join the groups at any time. Organizations such as Exodus (**www.exodus.co.uk**) offer this type of trip. While traveling in Peru, I had the pleasure of coming across an Exodus caravan, which moves around in trucks and buses. Just by chance, I ended up joining them; most people pre-book their trips. For the best information on overland tour operators, you can find information and a free e-book here:

https://blackfrogpublishing.wordpress.com/2014/01/12/the-ultimate-resource-for-overlanding-part-5-which-overland-company-should-i-go-with/

In Africa, overlanding often saves you a lot of hassle. I was in Zambia and had two weeks to spare, so I went to nearby Malawi using the scheduled overnight bus. When returning to Zambia to catch my plane, the bus service was canceled because there were not enough passengers. This meant making the journey with a few "minibuses". They are typically converted Mercedes-Benz vans accommodating three or even four rows of seats, plentiful everywhere in Africa. Nothing could have prepared me for the experience. We were squeezed like sardines into a van with music blasting from the speakers, complete with a failing starting engine. This was one of the roughest trips I had ever taken, but it was a typical travel day by Malawi standards.

The last minibus to the Zambian border decided to die en route (the second one that broke down that day) and the night was approaching, so from that point onwards it was "thumbs only." Hitchhiking is very popular in Africa. However, it is not free, as they expect some money in return for picking you up. I did not make it to the border that night, and my tourist permit expired that day.

It was a special permit I had obtained by bribing the officer, since I was not on the country list entitling me to a free visa. The following day the scene at the border was not a pretty one. The officer was shouting, I kept repeating the story, making it clear I had no more money to spare. After arguing for a while, he agreed to let me out of the country with a nasty passport stamp.

I understood then why so many people visiting Africa group together to buy a vehicle to travel in for a while. The journeys, although adventurous and colorful, can be nerve-wracking. What happened to me is typical and common; it can take forever to reach destinations, making following a timetable impossible. When you begin to enjoy making friends and experiencing the journey itself rather than the destinations, you will figure out ways to deal with the day-to-day, as well.

While traveling in the southern Indian state of Kerala, I stayed in a big colonial villa located in a tiny village. The owner was French and white; she had lived there for many years with her now teenage daughter who was schooled there. Aside from them, to find other westerners you would have to go to the closest city, which was thirty five miles away. She told me the locals never accepted her fully, not only because she was a foreigner but also because she was an emancipated woman in a country where a woman's role is limited to serving men. Despite the isolation and cultural clashes, she loved her life there. Her participation in the local community consisted primarily of empowering women who had been abused by their husbands.

This woman was a student, a performer, and a teacher of the fascinating local folklorist dance, Katakali. She also ran an import/export business and helped others with such businesses, always finding alternative ways to support herself and her daughter.

Was it easy? No. But was she special? No! "We sometimes underestimate how creative can be; as a species we are very adaptable," I remember her saying.

Another woman I met, an Australian in her forties, traded a career in advertising to embrace a nomadic lifestyle. I met her in Turkey during a total eclipse of the sun. She told me that for the past three years, her job had been to look after camels, nomadic animals in nature. Her duties consisted of moving around with them between Eastern Turkey and Iran. She became a woman of the desert, using the stars as a compass to direct her to the next oasis or Bedouin settlement. As I noticed her incredible insights derived not only from the experience of being with the camels, I told her she should write a book--equally to be treasured were her stories of the residents of remote communities she visited who offered her meals for the day and treated her as a sister despite her pale skin color. She had gained wisdom by contrasting western materialist values with a remote and deeply foreign culture. Possessions had little value for desert people, as they were often shared with whole communities.

These stories are unique, but what if there was a way to facilitate those extraordinary experiences? In one of my forthcoming books, I will explore this possibility in depth. Register your interest here.

www.goingnomadbook.com/upcoming

Finding The Nomad's Home

Your traveling pace will eventually slow down; travel can get tiring after a while, as previously stated. Sooner or later you will find a location that captivates you in a special manner—one that captures your curiosity or that you have simply fallen in love with— and you will find yourself toying with the idea of living there for a while.

Engaging in a new lifestyle and living in a foreign country takes time. Settling in rapidly can indeed happen if you allow yourself to be open enough so you can actively respond to challenges, perhaps using some of the suggestions below. The ideal is to have a balanced approach by relying not only on what I am saying here, but on your own wisdom and common sense.

If your destination is a big enough city, an established local system of finding jobs will be in effect, so it is a matter of finding out what you can do to navigate it. Similarly, providing a roof over your head can be relatively simple.

Some countries' visa requirements may not allow you to work, in which case you will likely be offered an "off the book" cash job (mostly underpaid). Cleaning, babysitting, waiting tables, casual construction and maintenance jobs are popular for nomads. Otherwise, you can earn remotely and pay your taxes in the country where you officially reside. (I know, after a while on the road it is hard to bear with bureaucracy!)

If, like me, you have lost interest in any type of urban environment, you still might find rural communities often do not welcome you at first. Organizing basic things, such as renting a house or finding work, can be challenging, especially if you have chosen a location almost virgin of foreigners or expats. This might not apply if this is your first trip and you have followed my advice to go away for just a year, in which case you might be so taken by your discoveries, feeling so excited, that finding a home is not required.

For all others, the first hurdle you are going deal with on your way towards leaving a footprint in your chosen idyllic setting consists of putting a roof over your head. It is time to decide how long you will stay in your future temporary abode, unless squatting in a shack would do it for you!

If you have a free-time schedule, keep it free: try not to rent anything for more than a six-month contract, so you can easily accommodate a move if you change your mind.

If this seems too long, consider three months as a minimum rental period. Although arranging a rental for shorter periods is possible, fewer people would be willing to offer you substantial savings for that length of time.

For nomads with an even shorter time span, the solution could be to barter below the asking price for whatever they find locally or to organize the rentals through hubs like **www.Airbnb.com**[6]. If not, housesitting or even couch surfing[7] can be an alternative.

As you may not find an opportunity in the exact dream location of choice, it helps to widen your search area a bit to increase your chances of finding a home. If that is your style, I suggest you begin by browsing the **http://www.workaway.info** website. Workaway has the biggest worldwide database of volunteer positions, including help in the house, eco projects, new age resorts, farms--the list is long. The length of stay varies from just weeks to yearlong positions, so you can fit them to any period length of time your stay might be.

If you do not find anything there, you can resort to the main method I am now going to suggest to everyone who is looking to find accommodations on longer terms. This is a traditional way of finding a temporary home, and is still a preferred way as it offers certainly more fun, although it requires skills to be mastered over time.

---

[6] *(an online global community marketplace, where regular folks generally rent either their spare room or entire houses)*

[7] *(this is where hosts allow guests to crash on their sofa for free for a while)*

What I am suggesting is to talk to locals--the tried and tested technique followed by realtors. This method requires boldness, a life asset essential to any reputable nomad.

If you find yourself in a faraway foreign culture, you have the advantage. Because people have a feeling of curiosity about you, approaching native people and starting a conversation, happens naturally with extreme ease. It is the "quest for the exotic" that you represent by being there that gets them interested in you. Learn, then to fulfill and exploit exactly that, cleverly using it to your own advantage.

(There are of course exceptions or degrees to which this quest applies to.)

The Magician warns you here to not overdo it:

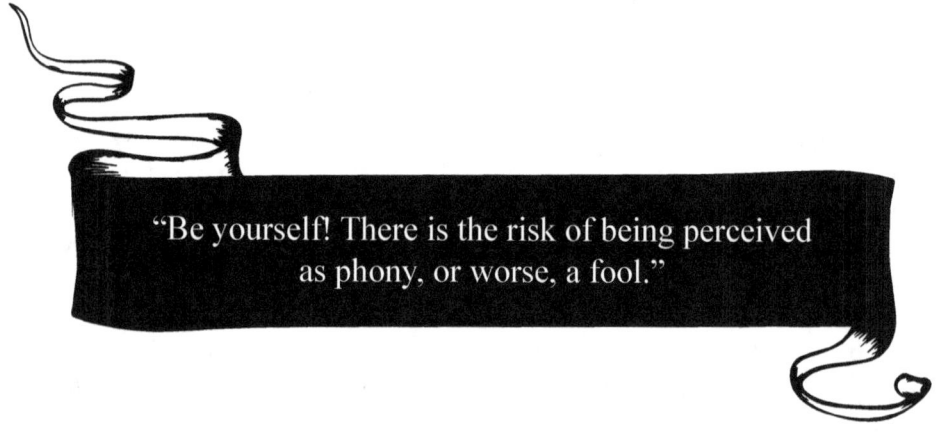

"Be yourself! There is the risk of being perceived as phony, or worse, a fool."

If that happens, you might have burned your chances; the naturally occurring attention will fade away due to your overindulgence.

Whenever you start a conversation with a local, before making requests, allow enough time to prompt their engagement with you first. You must show a genuine interest for what they tell or show you. You can quickly achieve that by asking them questions, elaborating on their answers with even more questions, and making sure they are aware you appreciate them. Sooner or later, they will ask the reason for your stay. This is when you say: "I have been traveling, but I have decided to stay here for a while. I like the people and the way of life very much, and would like to contribute to the community."

Pause. Wait to see if they say anything. Be ready to engage if they do. If not, you can add, "Unfortunately, I have not yet found any place to live. I don't know where to start." Pause. If they don't offer you any help then ask politely if they know of anyone renting a place, or how much you should expect to pay in that area.

It is quite likely they will help you straight away, or point you in the right direction; repeat with other people until you get somewhere. If you don't know the language, don't waste your time! Find an interpreter before you start this exercise, and pay them in the form of a meal/gift/wage according to what you might need them for. Chapter 8 deals in more detail with integrating yourself into the local culture; for now this is all you need to know.

Housekeeping

Once you have entered your newfound home, it makes sense to deal with organization and budgeting issues. Starting a household in a foreign location, although doable, takes time and hard work. Even if it seems you have a lot of money and you find you can easily afford to be there, why leave anything to chance? It is a good idea to figure out the cost of living as soon as you can by gathering enough information about:

- Wages
- Rent
- Transport
- Utilities
- Labor costs
- Food
- Clothing
- Local custom
- Neighbourly conduct (if it involves financial transactions)

All of this information can be obtained by talking to locals, even in the same conversation you had earlier to find the house. Start carrying a notepad with you at all times to write these costs and figures down. In another notepad, you can record the actual expenses for all of your purchases; this way you can always feel in control. I am confident that before you know it, you will work out a suitable strategy and adjust to changes with ease. Buying furniture makes sense only if you can quickly and easily sell it again. Otherwise, think in terms of borrowing, renting, or asking for them to be donated. If you can't imagine yourself taking advantage of pre-owned or recycled housewares, consider that traveling may teach you a lesson or two before you must make the decision!

Remember what I said in Chapter 3 about your inventory and cutting down on the material goods you currently have? If you have not done anything about it, yet, consider donating them to friends, charity, or complete strangers.

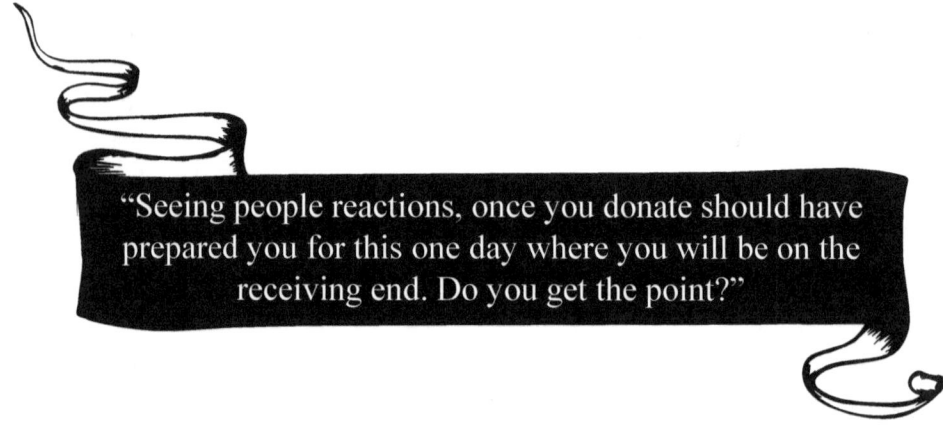

"Seeing people reactions, once you donate should have prepared you for this one day where you will be on the receiving end. Do you get the point?"

Everyday A New Day

Often, when you stop in a new place after having spent time traveling around, all of a sudden the days get longer.

This is not magic. It comes from the sudden change in pace, leaving a void to be filled with activities. A well-deserved physical rest can be one such activity; reading can be another. DIY projects in the house (if you rented one) can definitely be fun, even when you have never done it before. Find out what is going on in town from locals--show participation from the start; you will get more out of your visit if you do. Remember: you are a guest in their culture. Do not over-impose yours, or you risk being perceived as arrogant. Behaving like that might make some enemies and cause you trouble later on.

You can also take time to work on yourself, to improve your health for instance, or to deal with people and commitments you left behind.

This could be just a year break; if that is so, you might eventually go back. While you are away, there is nothing stopping you from contacting loved ones and dealing with past situations involving them remotely. You might have the time to reflect on many things regarding your life and simply want to make amends. Or, you might finally find the courage to say or come to terms with articulating what you previously did not have words for.

In the case of loved ones, use the phone or Skype instead of email or letters. Do not just write, as you might leave room for misunderstanding and compromise an eventual response.

There might well be other foreigners living in the neighborhood. Find them, ask why they ended up staying, how they did it, and if they have insights they would like to share with you. Keep their contact details somewhere and approach them any time something unusual happens or you don't know how to deal with a situation. Being a nomad cannot be pleasurable at all times--sometimes it's boring, sometimes stressful. When you come to a crossroads, your decisions might be critical, so practice asking for help when in doubt.

Having a mobile lifestyle does not mean escapism from yourself. What I mean is that sooner or later the personal issues you had at home might present themselves, even though the joy of traveling overshadowed them for a while. For the pleasure-seekers, this can be too much to figure out right now, as you have not gone yet on your trip. Believe in it is unnecessary; you can wait until you experience what I have just described. It will be a more powerful eye-opener that way because it will come from your own traveling wisdom. Expect to deal with it once you adjust to the new lifestyle and develop new habits as you accept the new standards.

The art of adapting to any situation is a nomad's joy. This includes your living habits and level of comfort. There is a very practical reason for this, which is that material things (tools, objects, services, and so on) might not be available where you go. On the other hand, there might be exciting new gadgets to try.

Using an analogy I made in an earlier Chapter as an example: the tropical pleasure of living on a hammock does have the advantage of being fully portable! I met plenty of people that only carry a small backpack and their hammock. This is mobility at its best. Happy, carefree people, who don't need four walls and who enjoy the shining stars as their roof.

For us folks with more traditional accommodation-standards, getting used to a new living condition can be somewhat challenging. My personal story can help you lighten up.

I Am Free I Love Being in Nature

Personally, I began my nomadic days by transitioning from city-living in a sterile, man-made jungle. There was one benefit to living in the city: it was largely an insect-free environment, and I hated insects! My dream was to get closer to nature; I soon realized I had to get over my fear of uninvited little beasts, but I did not know how to go about it.

That is, until, in the foothills of the Himalayas, I had my first "rebirthing" session. The technique requires the practitioner to cause an induced hypnotic state through a specific breathing rhythm. By doing so, the client will recreate the sensations he or she had at birth, as if consciously living the whole experience again. As I was waking up, after lying on a cushioned floor for almost an hour, I noticed a creepy crawler on my arm. I looked about, only to realize that the entire room was full of ants, worms, spiders, and other unidentified creatures.

I remained calm, communicating my disbelief to the smiley, turbaned man who was staring my way. He happily replied, "It is wonderful how many creatures were in God's original design!"

I embraced this new perspective, and from that day I have tried to remember it whenever I meet insects in my journeys. I am now emotionally immune to encounters with insects. I have survived a wasp-infested farm with ease, and on another occasion I had to share a room with a huge spider for an entire week. It was during a Buddhist retreat; in the tiny Spartan cell I slept in, I told the spider that I was not going to kill it and asked it if, for the time being, it would refrain from biting me. It worked!

The rule of not killing extended, in Buddhist fashion, to all living creatures. One day I had to apply it to a huge scorpion happily running in my direction. I captured it with a cup and carefully slid a piece of paper under its dangerous stinging tail and body, to avoid harm to either of us. The monks who taught me how to deal with an aggressive scorpion thought this process was not a big deal. For them, the danger it posed was totally void of the fear or drama that would normally be carried by any unfortunate disciple coming across such a fierce enemy.

According to the monk, it required a pragmatic and quick action, nothing else.

Having done it, yes, I can promise you can have a clear-headed approach to danger such as this. And just in case you face similar encounters, once captured, the scorpion must be taken as far away as possible from the living quarters. Scorpions do not like to be around people, so taking them away means they will never be back.

Living standards in certain places includes a good variety of animals as companions. The size of the houses can be smaller than what you are used to. I have lived in huts as well and it is fun. In a country like Thailand, most houses don't have a kitchen as everyone eats out. The mattress bed can be a bit hard and the standard can be well away from what you are used to in tropical places.

Once you get used to living quarters, the next task is to realize if the culture is one that lives more outdoors or indoors and to embrace it for a while. Experiment with all of the above; don't get overwhelmed, as you will adapt soon enough. There will be experiences you must accept and be open to. Do not jump out of a window, or get mad or angry--try to see things you are not used to with different eyes. Allow for a different perspective.

Once I arrived in South India and, after two days of hard traveling, I immediately rented a home-stay for a month. The room was beautiful, the family was nice, and the bathroom was in the yard. I took a shower and went to bed, as it was nighttime when I arrived. In the morning, I went to the outdoor toilet. It was one of those Asian squatting ones I had gotten accustomed to. As I was sitting down, I heard a loud "Oink, oink!" under my butt that tipped me.

The memories of the rebirthing man with the turban and his wisdom served little in keeping me calm, if you know what I mean. The piglets were waiting for breakfast! It sounds disgusting, but it is nature and nothing is wasted!

Those are the kind of fun or insane experiences you get up to live when becoming a nomad and free. Aren't they colorful?

Don't remain on the fence when feeling overwhelmed by those new and challenging occurrences that push you outside of your comfort zone or test your limits. Take them as an opportunity to practice something new that you simply did not understand well before. Greener pastures will always be seen if you look deep enough.

Getting closer to nature and adapting to simple living can be mastered quickly if you try. Those are skills you must have; otherwise, your wanting to see the world, your innermost desire to acquire nomadic wisdom, will lack of solid foundations: the essential skill-set.

In terms of meeting your needs, buy only little, asking yourself, "What is really essential?" This practice is best, as it makes it easier to keep moving after a few months are over. Do not accumulate stuff, as it turns into junk in no time. When traveling, learn to pack light and stay light as you progress.

Tips:

1) *If you meet on the road someone who has great valuable skills, get them to teach them to you. This will make you independent and very creative*
2) *Consider spending time working on a farm. If you don't have any experience in it, you will learn very useful skills.*
3) *Construction: You might one day want to build your own house, so if a fellow traveler needs a hand building a house, jump at the opportunity. Build it with them.*
4) *Do not end up working like you were at home, because the traveling lifestyle should be void of stress: keep it light.*
5) *Do plan for activities but don't leave too much time for doing nothing. It gets boring and believe it or not it is stressful.*

This was a chapter about adapting and taking your first steps in the place you will call home, even if in reality is a temporary arrangement. The road however, never ceases to surprise you and it might get soon get bumpy; read on to find out what I mean.

How To Deal With Problems Along The Way

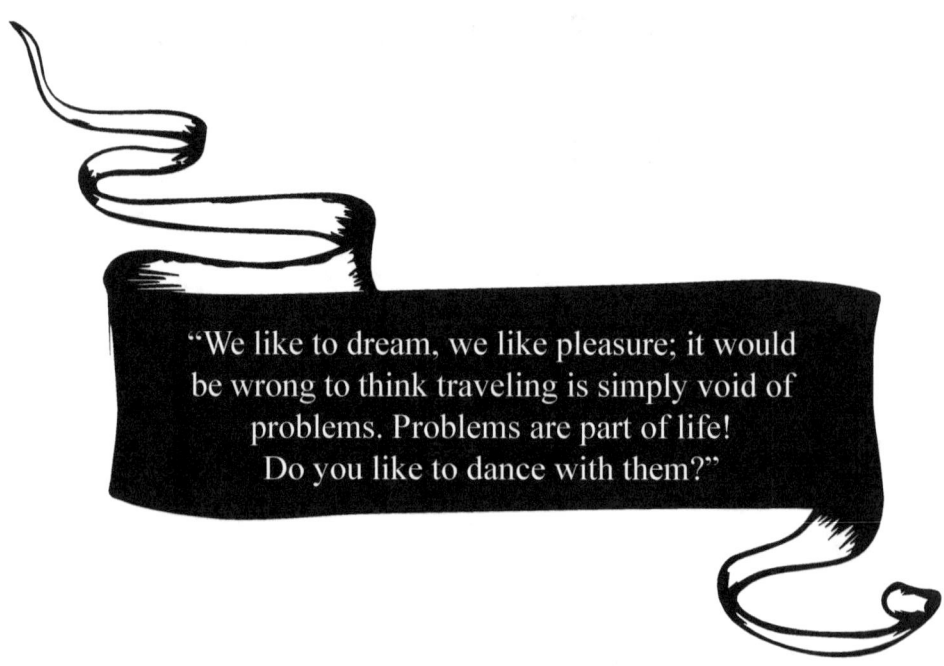

"We like to dream, we like pleasure; it would be wrong to think traveling is simply void of problems. Problems are part of life! Do you like to dance with them?"

After you have started to enjoy your new found freedom, and are having the time of your life, guess what? A problem arises out of the blue.

The Magician advises you to pay attention here.

Cultural Paradigm Treasures

Even in the nomad's carefree lifestyle, problems present themselves, offering an opportunity to learn new things and to become more confident.

One of the reasons seasoned nomads are amongst the wisest people on the planet is that they have dealt with a variety of problems. Along the way, they discovered creative solutions using their experience gained by having engaged with many different cultures.

Every culture has different traits, beliefs, values, and customs. As travelers, we do grasp them, even if at times we are not entirely conscious of this happening to us. Simply being exposed to a foreign culture for a certain length of time is enough to be personally influenced by it. We can then pick and choose from a series of new inherited references whenever we must interpret what happens around us or deal with problematic situations.

Having access to this new cultural spectrum is the source of the nomad's distinct insight. We are not meant to single our native culture out as the best there is or as the only one to draw from. The nomad can freely choose, without prejudice, what is the best reference to be used in a particular situation.

In this Chapter, I will attempt to give you examples of problems and ways to deal with and solve them. I use a combination of common sense and experience. As discussed in previous Chapters, being flexible and prepared are the skills required of you to make progress; in shaky situations, nothing, however, will replace your own cultural openness. Once you learn to deal with problems in such a broad, enlightened manner during your traveling career, and, if you continue this lifestyle, then the Magician will reward you with a certificate in Wisdom Mastery!

Give a high-five to the Magician, please—his hand is waiting!

Before listing the types of problems you are most likely to confront, let's reiterate the flexibility issues, such as the different living standards and lack of comfort that you are used to. Since you are in an unfamiliar place, the things you are accustomed to are nowhere to be found. This factor plays a part with problem solving, too. Being in this foreign environment might make us react slowly in the presence of danger. Flexibility in this context means to be able to recognize, quickly and reliably, people who can help us.

When you meet new people, see how they can be useful--don't just go with the "like or don't like" type of assessment. The more people you are able to communicate with, the better, as their skills might be useful one day. This does not mean you should be an opportunist, just practical. While it is good practice to record the name and contact details of a person you have just met, don't stop there. Put a note next to their name and add what they do and how they might be useful in the future. Pay attention when people tell you stories, as they can carry information for this purpose.

Practice flexibility when you find yourself in situations that challenge your belief systems. You might struggle to understand or realize that your approach will not be practical or can be misinterpreted. See if somehow you can grasp the other cultural point of view and learn to empathize.

A typical example is when your partner is of a different culture and nationality. You have to put extra effort into understanding each other in order to communicate effectively and make sure there are no misunderstandings. Similarly, when you are in a foreign culture, learning to see through a new cultural lens takes practice. In

Chapter 8, I will give a few communication examples.

There was a time in my nomadic career that taught me to listen carefully and to act in a way that was not so compliant with my quiet, non-confrontational nature. At that time, I enjoyed spiritual shopping and ended up spending time with shamans[8].

Once upon a time. . . There was a shaman in Bali, a Hindu island in Indonesia. There were close to thirty westerners staying in his dwelling. This was a farmhouse, set on the mystical foothill of Mount Agung, an impressive dormant volcano dominating the landscape of this magical island.

An envious, powerful local shaman claimed territorial rights and threatened to attack the ashram[9] with his Balinese followers. He was somehow under the impression that we had been paying money, making our shaman rich while he got nothing. He was eager to demand settlement. It was like a declaration of war.

While our shaman was getting ready with his negotiation speech, we had to find a way to defend the ashram from any possible attack. We quickly had to learn some of the symbolism of Balinese culture, which is mostly non-violent but visually fierce. If they saw us ready, acting not as typical western tourists but instead keeping an integrated appearance and showing a grasp of Balinese ways of handling things, they would recognize a much more powerful enemy. This would grant us bargaining power.

We created an impromptu theatrical stage set, from the clothes we wore, to our facial expressions, to what we carried in our hands. We had to learn to perform it in time for the arrival of the shaman and his followers.

When the enemies arrived, we allowed their shaman inside while we remained standing tall by the closed gate that separated us from the followers on the other side. Not a word was uttered, total silence. The two groups looked constantly into each other's eyes. Inside, the negotiation between the two shamans went well as they established territorial boundaries and other details. Outside, we were confronting each other: the silence continued between the two platoons, communicating wordlessly in distant warfare. Eventually the group on the other side of the gate began to retreat, well before their shaman returned with an agreement.

What happened? In reality, they came in not to engage in battle but to make us afraid of an attack. However, they saw that their fear tactics did not work. So, admitting defeat, they retreated.

Teachers cannot always be present to make you part of the culture. For us, this was a lesson from the inside using a Balinese defense tactic. It is exotic and far removed from my culture and that of most the readers of this book.

---

[8] *Local traditional healers from indigenous cultures*

[9] *Hindu meditation and yoga center*

Because we were a group made entirely of westerners, I could see that many of us wanted to use our own forms of response to this situation. Instead, we agreed to act with conviction according to the paradigm of the other culture. Goofy copycats? Perhaps. I can only say that it worked. This would have been unlikely in the scenario if we kept acting from our own belief system.

Common Types of Problems

The story I have shared is quite unusual, and you are unlikely to find yourself in a war between shamans. However, you might find yourself in the middle of a political revolution, or a major socio-economic change. The best strategy in those cases is certainly repatriation. But in case that might not be possible, learn as much about local customs as possible and you will be just fine, even when the embassy or consulate is far away.

Here are more common types of problems that most of us encounter sooner or later in our travels:

- Accidents
- Health
- Relationship
- Legal
- Work

A good travel insurance should cover all health and legal risks (including emergency air ambulance). One that pays providers directly, instead of reimbursing your charges, is the wisest of all preventive measures. Although it is unlikely to happen, anything that will keep your life out of danger is worth paying and planning for.

Accidents

When dancing away under the coconut trees, who knew that one of those trees was going to fall in the middle of the dance floor. Many were trapped under it, including a Dutch girl who went under. She was taken, unconscious, to the local hospital where she might have had little chance of survival. Since she had the proper insurance, an air ambulance was organized so she could be transferred to Holland. She received a lifesaving operation that was not even dreamed of in the country where she was happily dancing under the stars.

It is far more common to have an "accident-free" traveling career. Having witnessed few unfortunate incidents such as the one described above, however, I would not consider traveling without travel insurance. Less dramatic incidents such as non-life-threatening motorbike accidents can be common in places. Check with the locals to see if the statistics are high, in which case think twice and be extra careful in those towns. If you rent a scooter or a bike, always make sure they are insured, as some countries do not require this or fail to include it in the hiring rate.

Other problems occur during outdoor activities including hiking, scuba diving, rafting, or snowboarding. But any type of sport can be dangerous; accidents are not limited to risky ones.

Adventure itineraries and tours are very popular with all nomads, not just the young ones. Somehow, these have become bonding rituals as well as tools for self-discovery and growth. A book might be needed to describe the vast array of breakthroughs and potentially life-changing experiences such activities might provide. They offer an opportunity to challenge fears and phobias, to push boundaries, and to break limiting beliefs. They do indeed strengthen courage; "Turning People into Unstoppable Lions!" could well be the promise advertised in a brochure of such activities. I often see a good ratio of delivery on that promise from people who take part in adventures. It is worth considering them and not giving up because you fear something bad might happen to you; just have the right level of coverage in your travel insurance and be prepared.

Health

While serious accidents are rare, sickness and disease are more frequent travel companions. We are more susceptible to disease in a foreign environment because of changes in lifestyle and eating habits, as well as our lack of antibodies to local germs.

Prevention is crucial to maintaining your health while traveling. Pay attention to washing your hands and making sure raw food is properly washed. Eat freshly cooked food and avoid buffets where food is left out for a while. Drink bottled water, even when the tap water is drinkable and safe. You might drink it later on if you wish, when your body is fully adjusted to the environment.

Dehydration is common if you travel at a fast pace. Remember to keep your body hydrated, especially if you are in a climate different from the one at home. Remembering to drink water will help you to adjust quickly and reduce jet lag. Be aware that you will need more rest than normal when you travel. All of this advice can be found in any traveler's guide if you require more tips. What you are not going to find in most guides is the following information about how to de-tox, and even de-worm, hinted in a previous Chapter. Most detox products not regulated by the FDA; the information below is my own opinion and results may vary.

Detoxing is very popular these days. Travelers have been using it for decades as a safe method to stay well. You don't need to wait until you are feeling sick to detox and cleanse, ridding your body of any excess toxins it has accumulated. However, detoxing is not without risk. Our bodies are designed to eliminate toxins efficiently on a daily basis and cannot safely expel more than they already do. It can be dangerous to put the body through unnecessary stress, and you may damage a very delicate balance. Medical professionals disagree on this; some say that for a short period of time, the body can safely undertake the stress of eliminating even more toxins.

Despite the risks, fasting, cleansing, and detoxing have become a lucrative business. Many places that offer these techniques are dangerous because of inadequate or completely useless residential programs. Word of mouth is still the best method to get recommendations of a program, book, or holistic practitioner who has mastered this methodology, making it safe and very effective.

I invite you to do your own research on the subject. If you want to contact me about this or anything else in this book, please do so using my website. You never know; if there are enough of you, I may organize a Going Nomad readers' forum or detox retreat, as it is one of my areas of expertise.

Of course there are ways to detox entirely by yourself by purchasing an internal "cleansing kit". What works best, however, is to take at least three weeks (four is even better) to follow specific diets—fasting, juicing, and raw food, as well as regularly cleaning the bowels with self-administrated enemas. You can eliminate toxins through sweat too, by using any kind of sauna or steam room (I recommend using infrared saunas), gentle forms of exercise, or balanced herbs and supplements. Also, be sure to use relaxation, meditation, and forms of introspective work such as journaling. In any reputable residential program, educational lectures on healthy nutrition habits will also be offered.

The combination of these approaches gives you a full initiation into becoming your own physical Magician. Learn your body's alchemy and feel radiant with boundless energy.

De-worming is another very popular healthcare regimen amongst the Japanese, who have a lot of raw fish in their diet. Westerners also used to do it in the past, but we lost the habit. I recommend de-worming twice a year; it involves taking some prescription tablets and is painless. Untreated worms, amoebas, and other uninvited guests can cause many problems. Because worms tend to remain undiagnosed, they can be there for a long time. Regularly practicing de-worming avoids this risk (no harm in trying!) and we might also feel much better later.

If we chose to pay attention to our health by preventing disease, it is unlikely we are even going to catch the flu. The traveling community is full of very healthy and radiant people. You will meet them on the road, so ask their secrets and before you know it, you might be one of them.

Become knowledgeable about your environment. The local flora might be used medicinally, but some of the plants and herbs might be toxic. The same applies to the fauna: some of the animals around might be dangerous. Learn how to capture a scorpion, if that is a danger there. Have the right spider/snake antidote stored in your house and know where to go if you get bitten. Avoid touching stray dogs and cats, as they might be sick or carrying fleas. You can also invest in a first aid course if you have time on your hands (especially before you go traveling). You will learn a good deal, and first aid training is a skill for life.

Relationships

Problems in relationships can be hard to plan for or to prevent; they just happen with whoever is traveling with you or as you meet new people.

If you are in a relationship, even if your other half is elsewhere, travel is likely to bring some changes to the relationship. Traveling long-term changes you, sometimes drastically, so any bond in your relationship will be tested. The most common conflict is that very often you and your partner disagree about location or have different preferences for activities or traveling styles. If you cannot reach an agreement, it is better to part temporarily, do what you each want to do, then touch base at a later time. If you have followed my guide, you already know the how-to for this. There is no reason to have a falling out, just trust the process.

In other cases, your partner might reveal traits that change the dynamic of the relationship and invite you to further reflection. Can you live with the changes? Are you still compatible? If not, is it time to end it? Remember that travel is a challenge for everyone: if you end it, agree to meet in a year to see if the incompatibility was real or just a result of temporary travel-related stress.

If you just met your partner in your travels, very often infatuation takes over. When travel plans do clash, usually one of the two agrees to follow the other person's itinerary. This is quite dangerous as it backfires in the first few arguments with the partner. You need a lot of understanding to make a travel romance last.

As for friends and traveling companions, relationship problems can be easier to deal with. You will soon learn to bond with strangers in a very short time and then be ready to say goodbye, sharing a tear or two and knowing you will never meet again.

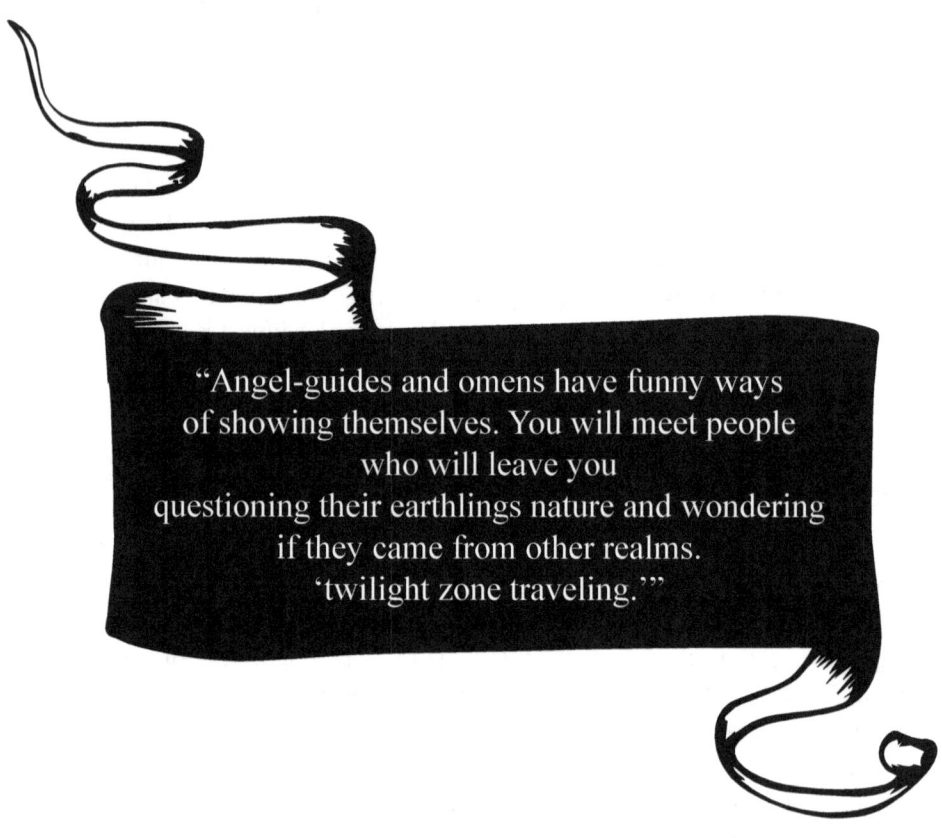

"Angel-guides and omens have funny ways of showing themselves. You will meet people who will leave you questioning their earthlings nature and wondering if they came from other realms. 'twilight zone traveling.'"

Legal and Work

There might be a number of legal issues covered by your travel insurance. However, the world seems to be very unfair in places. In some countries, being a foreigner puts you automatically in the weaker seat of any legal case. Your case does not have to go to extremes (such as being caught with illegal drugs in a country where the offense carries the death penalty). Even for lesser offenses, prosecution and sentencing can determine harsh punishment simply based on the culture your passport citizenship represents. Exceptional cases cause widespread controversy. Human rights activists and the media will often deal directly in those circumstances.

I remember seeing an Australian TV mini-series called "Better Man."[10] It was a true story of an unfortunate drug mule caught in Singapore and eventually hanged. I recommend you watch it if you can; it is an eye opener on clashing cultural belief systems and the lack of internationally recognized universal human rights.

The disadvantage of being a foreigner can affect smaller cases too. Most people tend to leave the country before any legal proceedings if they perceive they will be treated unfairly.

The most common legal issues are overstaying work permits. I cannot enter into a debate that promotes illegal activities. So if you are considering overstaying a work permit or visa, I can only suggest making it as legal as possible and weighing any consequences of being caught in advance.

Some countries have a relaxed attitude to overstaying. Usually you can legally do a "visa run" or get passport stamps simply by leaving the country and getting back in again in a single day. This is popular in some Asian and Latin American countries. In the West, especially, there might be a maximum days in a calendar year you are allowed to stay. Some countries might throw you out and ban you from returning in the future if you get caught overstaying.

In India and Latin America, I have met several fugitives and illegal residents who have managed to stay for many years. However, this sacrifices their nomadic mobility, as they cannot leave the country or cross any border without consequences. If they do decide to leave, they usually claim that they have lost their passport, so they won't appear to have been staying indefinitely.

Work permits are very difficult to define. A good lawyer seems always able to navigate the system, finding loopholes in the law to help you stay in case you get caught working without a permit, or helping you to get your papers in order.

In talking to locals and expats, you might discover local customs that are common practice and replace, or work alongside, the country's immigration laws. You will also be made aware of how long it will take for you to become legal. Employers, at times, are useful allies to get you established.

In this chapter, we have looked at problems that can happen on the road. As I said, they are opportunities in disguise to make us better people by giving us a great deal of wisdom. My suggestion is to deal with them directly, even if a change of scenery is required or if you are tempted instead to give in to escapism, thinking it as an easier route.

If you don't deal with these problems, they might get bigger and present

---

[10] *SBSTV Better Man, is based on the true story of Van Tuong Nguyen, a 25-year-old Vietnamese-Australian man who was arrested in Singapore, convicted of drug trafficking and sentenced to the death penalty in 2005.*
The series follows the story of a young man who had a tough but loving upbringing with his twin brother and devoted mother. The story culminates in an extraordinary three-year legal battle to save the life of Nguyen, led by Julian McMahon, a Melbourne lawyer, and Lex Lasry QC, a Melbourne barrister.

themselves at a later time in a nastier fashion. I believe that if a problem shows itself, we will be ready to deal with it--so just having enough courage to "face the music" always pays off at the end. My aim was not to include all problems, just the most common and to provide you with a general insight into dealing with all sort of unexpected scenarios.

In the next Chapter, I will introduce one other problem of a different kind. Sometimes when we depart, we leave something behind that we cannot avoid dealing with, or else a special occasion arises out of the blue. They could be so important that a trip home is needed. Yes, regrettably, it is sometimes necessary to cut your trip short or take a break from it. There are ways to not let this be a trip-spoiler, so let's try to turn this into a positive rewarding experience.

Chapter 7

When the nomad Must go home

"There's no place like home,"
John Howard Payne

"Years have gone by. You flow beautifully. Your eyes twinkles. An unlikely sage in the making you are. Those gifts are for you to guard and keep safe throughout this lifetime. Make no mistake, they belong to the universe, not you! You cannot stop change. You may pack one last time--that day will arrive eventually. It is not a sad day; it is a day when something else is just beginning…"

For many, a nomadic way of life seems like it would be exhilarating. For others, it's completely absurd, and then there are the nomads themselves who simply see this as their way of life.

For years, you've been jumping from one place to another, taking in all the sights. Squatting, camping, and living off the earth without any "real" place to call home. But there always comes a time, whether you want to or not, when you've got to bite the bullet and return home—as in the place where you were born or the place where your family lives. It's been a couple of years since you've been home and you haven't seen anyone from your past for a long time, so you have to expect things will be different--very different.

The nomadic life, when the intrepid traveler flits from one place to another with very little aim, is a lifestyle choice. It's not for everyone--that's for sure-- but for those who aren't interested in planting their roots anywhere in particular and settling down, this is ideal–for many, it's a lifelong vacation. When it comes time to pack up your meager belongings and to head home for some reason or other, it can be daunting.

Different reasons you might take the trip home

Nomads, or travelers, have to face going home for a number of reasons. They could be happy occasions; they could be sad occasions; they could be obligatory family commitments that you just can't escape. Or perhaps it's got something to with the pile of debt you left behind. Sometimes you just can't get out of it despite your million-and-one protests and excuses. Yes, it's time to go home.

It can be slightly daunting to think about having to go home. It's scary, especially after you've been out of the loop for a while. At some points you may even dread facing the things that you haven't had to deal with for so long. That fear, coupled with a little bit of excitement, will send your head into a bit of a spin.

One of the biggest reasons why many nomads have to make the trek home is family-related issues. Some nomads actually choose to escape reality because of family, but like the old saying goes:

"You can choose your friends, but you can't choose your family," which is why nomads have to face reality and go home sometimes. Your family is always going to be there and at some point they're going to need you. They may need you to support them through a tough period they're going through, such as a divorce or death. They may need you to come back and help take care of an elderly relative. They may need you to help come back and look after a sick family member... Whatever it is, your family needs you and it's really difficult to say "no."

Another common reason why nomads have to venture home after living their life of simplicity elsewhere is death. A death of a family member or a close friend will often bring nomads out of the woodwork from all around the world. Ridden with guilt and shame for not having kept in better contact, a death will bring the prodigal child back home. It's a morbid reason to visit, but for many it's their chance to pay their last respects. If it's someone close to you, often you'll be asked to come home earlier to help with funeral arrangements and other preparations.

Illness in the family is yet another reason why the nomad will sigh, pack their bags, and make the trip home again after such a long time. Obviously, you're not going to be running home for a runny nose or a broken leg, but there are times when serious illnesses strike you or a family member.

Perhaps your family has asked you to come home, or it could be that you've made the decision to head home alone–you can't face another guilty conscience. However, imagine if the tables turned and it were you who needed your family-- they'd drop everything and help you, despite your "unorthodox"lifestyle choices. Caring for a sick family member is an obligation, and in a way, you owe this to your family. Perhaps you need to meet with your family to determine which medical procedure is best. Perhaps you've got to make the decision as to who is going to pay for the care. At the end of the day, it's your duty to go home to spend time with a sick family member... Life's too short--you just never know!

But it's not all doom and gloom when you go back home. Sometimes you can throw on your glad rags and some dancing shoes and go home for a fun event, such as special family occasions that can't be missed. Do you really want so-and-so whispering about you and questioning why you have yet again chosen to decline an invite? Weddings, engagement parties, graduations, and baptisms are just a few of the joyous occasions that draw the prolific traveler back to their roots. Obviously, if you get invited by your old neighbor to his daughter's wedding and you haven't seen them for ten odd years, you'll probably decline. But if Granny Dot and Grandpa Joe are celebrating their fiftieth wedding anniversary and their wish is for their reckless grandchild to come home for it, you're under some duress to accept the invite--even if it means having to listen to hours of speeches about your boring family history and sitting next to your alcoholic great uncle who lost his marbles a while back.

Your heart may be another thing that hauls you home. If you're in a long-distance relationship and you or your partner is struggling with the conditions, then one of you is going to have to give in and sacrifice a little. That is most likely going to be the nomad because if your partner were really willing to follow you and your nomadic lifestyle, they would be doing so already. If you choose to keep your long-distance relationship going while you hop from city to city and country to country, you need to make sure you understand one thing: maintenance. This maintenance has nothing to do with a broken pipe, a leaking faucet, or mowing the lawns; it's related to relationship maintenance. To be able to keep your relationship healthy, you need to work at it. And that means you, the nomad, the traveler of the world, must constantly go home to touch base with your loved one. If you don't do this, your relationship will simply fizzle and die.

If it's been a while since you last went home to see your partner, you've got

to make it up to them. This is your sole purpose for putting your feet on your homeland soil again and don't forget it. You were part of the decision-making process of getting involved in a long-distance relationship; your partner did not tie you down and force you into it because if this was the case, you wouldn't still be living the nomadic lifestyle. If you want to make this work, it's up to you.

On the subject of partners, but of a less favorable kind, your ex could be a reason why you have to touch base. No doubt this meet is one you'd rather not have— they're called an ex for a reason, right? Sometimes this needs to be done, so there's no more burying your head in the sand. It's even more imperative that you get home if there are kids involved—is it really fair not to visit your kids just because you've separated from your partner? Your visit home could simply be catching up with your kids and spending some quality time with them before you jet off once again. It could be to sort out papers and other exhausting legal documents, such as child support or divorce papers. It could be that your ex is so sick and tired of seeing all your "junk" (as they call it) piling up in the garage that they're threatening to throw it all out if you don't come home and sort it out. Whatever the reason for having to go home because of your ex-partner, you've got to go in with a open mind, maintain your ground, and exercise patience--because you're going to need it.

Just thinking about lawyers, solicitors, and courts can make you never want to return home. But if you've got unfinished legal business back in your home state, you've got to sort it out. Otherwise, things could begin to slowly get out of control, especially if there are unpaid monies involved--all of a sudden, you've got a massive debt and a huge black mark against your name. If you have children back home with an ex, it's your duty to pay child support every month and if you don't, you'll be slapped with a huge fine and a court order. The same goes for taxes and unpaid bank loans or overdraft fees. Get your finances sorted – get home, make a plan, and figure out how you're going to pay it back while being a nomad. Other legal reasons why you might need to go home for a bit is for a hearing of a will–you don't want to miss out on the small fortune that Great Aunt Poppy left you, do you?

In some cases, it might be that you don't have anywhere to base yourself in the meantime. It could be that you're on a long-term leave from work, or possibly you've lost your previous job and you're now unemployed. If this is so, you'll most likely consider going home for a short period of time and, much to your dismay, lodge with your parents or relatives for a short while until more concrete work comes your way.

It's really difficult being unemployed these days and this is the time where you're going to literally have to count every dime because you don't really have a clear idea when your next paycheck will come in. Another scenario might be the whole visa-thing. If you've been residing abroad and want to apply for a visa, some countries actually require you to apply for this outside of the country, which would mean you heading home until all the bureaucrac and paperwork is fulfilled and you've got a new shiny visa stamp in your bulging passport again.

Planning a trip home

As wonderful and as great as it sounds, you can't just pack up your things like you've been doing and head home. It's time to not think like a nomad and now be a little bit more realistic. It's time to get organized and really think about what is involved when it comes to going home whether it is a short-term trip or a more permanent one. You're going to have people fighting over you. People who you haven't seen or heard from, for literally ages, will be begging for you and expecting you to drop by. Many people will have high expectations of your visit home, and just thinking about all the possible family engagements that your mom's been secretly plotting is enough for you to think about ripping up your ticket and saying, "Next year!"

But that next year will roll into another year and then another – you get the picture. The longer you leave this hotly anticipated trip home, the more expectations people are going to have of you when you do get around to visiting. Avoid people pressuring you and all that extra-added stress by getting organized. And a great way of really killing this and making sure you stay on task is by writing lists, lots of lists.

If you're not a list person, you're going to become one. Lists help you figure out what it is you need to do. Lists will help you figure out what it is you want to do, and of course, what you don't want to do. Lists will become your new best friend and as soon as you begin to see the positive changes that lists will have in your life, you'll become slightly obsessed and write lists for absolutely everything. When you write them, you'll be able to prioritize better–do you really need to visit your mom's best friend in the care home? Make sure you allocate times as well. If you don't specify timeframes, you could totally lose sight of what it is you're supposed to be doing and you'll end up spending too much time on something menial and running out of time for something more important.

Don't forget your goals. What do you want to achieve while you're back? For sure, you're going to be trying to please others by doing as much as you can, but if you forget the reason why you're there in the first place, you're just going to end up leaving unfulfilled. What are your expectations? Writing down what you expect will prepare you for things – the good, the bad, and the ugly. Writing lists isn't just for the super organized or the geek; it's for anyone (including the nomad) who wants a successful trip home.

You always have to bear in mind that your time is limited, therefore precious. This is why you need to keep it realistic and always remember why you're making the trip home in the first place.

Remember it's necessary to be a little selfish at times. Plan some alone time.

It's important to plan some "me" time so you don't get burned out. You'll easily
It's important to plan some "me" time so you don't get burnt out. You'll easily become overwhelmed and stressed once all those invites come flowing in and many people start fighting over who's going to serve you their favorite pot roast on Sunday night–this is what headaches are made of and it'll have you reaching for the nearest beer or other alcoholic beverage. Forget the beer and plan some alone-time. Figure out what you're going to do before you go so that you don't waste any of that precious time while you're there. It's really important that you get the chance to recharge your batteries, otherwise you'll become tired. And when you're tired, you'll be irritable and stressed and you'll also have a lesser chance of achieving your goals.

Dealing with loved ones

Loved ones--they could be your immediate family members, your extended ones, and close friends. These people have impacted your life somehow and over the years they're still present in your life. A loved one is not a cousin you fell out with years ago. Just because someone is a family member, it doesn't give them the natural rite of passage to be classified as your loved one. A loved one is a person you still are close to, someone you care about, someone who hasn't harmed or hurt you. A loved one is person who's always around when you do venture home. No matter what, you'll always love these people and they'll always love you; however, this might be difficult to recognize.

The thing is, you've changed. There's no doubt about it and I'm not referring to the massive unruly beard you've grown on your face. Other than a few physical changes, you've changed as a person–your values, your beliefs, your priorities. Be prepared for the obvious questions of "Why?" "Why do you continue to waste your life wandering about?" "Don't you think it's time you settled down somewhere, anywhere?" Here's the thing, no matter what, there are always going to be those people who just don't get you and have a hard time understanding the new you. They're confused and they don't understand your new lifestyle, and for this reason they're having a hard time respecting it. Perhaps you haven't changed for the worse, but they remember the old you. Many people are quite stuck in their ways and don't respond well to change, and simply put they prefer the old you!

You may experience your loved ones acting weird. They may not know what to say. Basically, it's going to take them time to adjust and to get used the idea that you're no longer the same person you were before. Instead of getting all defensive regarding your choice to become a nomad in a heated debate, be patient. This is when you're going to have to exercise good listening skills. Listen to what they have to say and take all those snarky comments with a pinch of salt. Eventually they're going to come around, so just wait it out and if they don't, don't sweat it. This is who you are now and they have to accept you for who you are, warts and all.

Your loved ones are going to do one of two things. Either they're going to chew your ear off and talk to you until the cows come home, or they're going to remain quiet. It's most likely going to be the former and you're going to have to put up with a lot of nonsense and crap. Again, exercise your patience and allow them to talk. Just like you have the right to do what you want, they have the right to say what they want everyone's entitled to an opinion. Respect what they have to say and fight the urge to swear and argue back. Just let them speak (you don't even have to listen) to avoid any argument because, let's face it, you're only home for a short period of time and you don't know when you're going to see them again, so what's the point in arguing?

.Just because you're listening to them doesn't mean that you have to change and give into their desires. Stand your ground and say "no" if that's what you really want. You don't need to agree with everything and everyone. Yes, you may be showing them respect by opening your ears and listening to them babble away, but you also have to be strong and firm and this means saying "no" with a certain conviction.

Obviously, if you just turn around and say "no" without explanation, people are going to point the finger and basically you'll have confirmed their suspicions that you've changed. Don't give them the pleasure of being right. Instead you have to be bigger than them and explain your reasoning behind the simple two-letter word of refusal. You can't please everyone--that's impossible. And you can't play God, which is why you also can't be in a number of different places at once – you don't have a clone or clones, so this is going to be your main argument. Kindly explain to them (without losing it) that you have limited time. Promise them that you'll stay in touch (be prepared to be met with rolling eyes) and that's that. C'est la vie, this is life. Make them feel appreciated, and show them respect and how much you care about them. In some cases, you're going to have to bend and compromise–you can't go home without visiting your brother or sister, but for others it's going to be much easier.

Whatever happens, don't get sucked in. Family members and loved ones have a knack for making you feel guilty when you shouldn't. There will be some family members in particular, like your mom, who are going to be a little bit more manipulative. They're going to do little things, cunning things and will try to trick you into staying. Mom might cook you your favorite dishes every night of the week–she's trying to show you that you don't get such good home-cooking where you are. Dad might buy you a couple of tickets to go and watch your favorite team play. Your friends might throw crazy parties in your honor, just like those you used to have in the old days. Be warned: these may be ways of welcoming you home, but they're also ways of trying to trick you and getting you to stick around. You'll start thinking, "Oh, this is nice." "I could move back for this." These thoughts are just an illusion. They're temporary feelings. You already feel vulnerable and emotional about having to make the trip back home, so don't be fooled. Make sure you remain true to your cause, stand your ground, and be vigilant; tell yourself, "This is a temporary visit and nothing else."

On the other hand, you might have a Dorothy moment like in the Wizard of Oz and realize that there really is "no place like home." Deciding to stay is not a huge deal. If this is what you want, so be it. It's completely fine and no one's going to judge you or gossip behind your back. It could be that your nomadic way of life was just a temporary thing; it was an experience that you had, and it was a great period of time for soul-searching. Perhaps you feel like you've really grown. You've finally found yourself during your time away from home, which is why you've decided you want to stay. For sure you're going to feel pangs of guilt for leaving your old nomadic life behind you, but treasure the experiences you had instead. You'll also feel confused and you'll continuously be plagued with the same question, "Is this the right decision for me?"

Confusion is normal especially since the last few years had been dedicated to the nomadic lifestyle. Confusion can just add to the stress of things and if you don't control it, you're going to feel an overwhelming sense of panic. A great and easy way to combat this is through journaling. Write down absolutely everything, from your thoughts, to your desires, to your worries and concerns. When a person is confused, they have the tendency to make rash decisions. Those on-the-spot decisions sometimes work out and at other times they don't, which is why journal writing helps–it gives you the chance to have afterthoughts and avoid making any flippant, rushed decisions. Journal writing will allow you to be more realistic without your emotions getting in the way of things. After gathering all your thoughts, ideas, frustrations, and fears, you might end up realizing that you really do want to stay, which is perfectly cool. If you're really at a loss about what to do, contact your friends; find other nomads in the same situation and get some advice.

Reasons for the nomad to stay

"Maybe you had to leave in order to really miss a place; maybe you had to travel to figure out how beloved your starting point was."

Jodi Picoult (Handle With Care)

Life as a nomad doesn't necessarily mean being a tripper or a wanderer for the rest of your life. Some things come to an end. Sometimes you grow out of things. Sometimes, other things become more important to you. Sometimes you just tire of the adventure and of the unknown and dream of more stability, even if it is somewhat boring. Whatever your reason is to stay, it's your business--but just make sure you're doing it for the right reasons. Make sure you're doing it for you and no one else.

One of the biggest reasons to stay is your love life. Life as a nomad definitely has its perks, but it also has some drawbacks too. The biggest one is loneliness. Some people move away from home and turn to the nomadic life because this is what they crave. But as humans, we all need to feel loved.

On your recent trip back home, you may realized that your partner, who you've been in a long-distance relationship with, is really the one for you. You've finally realized that you need to return home if you really want to make things work. Your time away from home was rewarding, but now you've gained more insight--you feel like it's time to settle down a bit and perhaps start a real family of your own... Like a real grown-up. You've realized that even though they didn't want to join in on your worldly adventures, they're really for you. They remained loyal and waited for you, and now it's time for you to make a few sacrifices and compromises too.

Perhaps one of the reasons why you decided to take off into the unknown in the first place was because of a broken heart. Your ex broke it off and left you broken. Not being able to face them and seeing them around town made you pack up your few things and head off into the wild. Upon returning, you may meet with your ex and, basically, the love is still there. Absence has made the heart grow fonder and now that you've grown and found yourself, you can also see that you too made a few mistakes. You've chatted about it and you've decided that you're both willing to make a real effort. This is something you shouldn't feel guilty about because everyone deserves love and happiness and if this is what you want, so be it!

When deciding to stay, make some more lists. Weigh up those pros and cons and see where your heart and feelings lie. Be honest with yourself.

Ask yourself, "Is this really something I want?" Talk things through; continue to journal and think about things really carefully. Don't be fooled by emotional blackmail and sexual desire. Are you just hanging around longer in order to avoid saying goodbye? What's the point in this? Sooner or later you're going to have to say "bye," and the longer you leave it, the harder it will get. No one can make the decision for you. It's one-hundred percent up to you.

Seasoned nomads usually avoid going home for many reasons. Mainly because of all the politics and emotions involved and the games that people play. Nomads leave home to fulfill simpler lives without the constant telephone calls from their mom checking up on them despite them being thirty years old or even older. Just because you give yourself up to the nomadic way of life doesn't mean that you're chained to it forever–it's not a convent or a monastery. For some nomads, it's their destination and just because they've chosen this life away from home doesn't mean they have things to hide. Like in JRR Tolkien quote I used earlier, "Not all who wander are lost." Some will continue to wander and some will finally head home after many years of being away, but whatever you choose, you're always going to have to go home at some stage.

Chapter 8

The expat experience
Going Global without Going Crazy

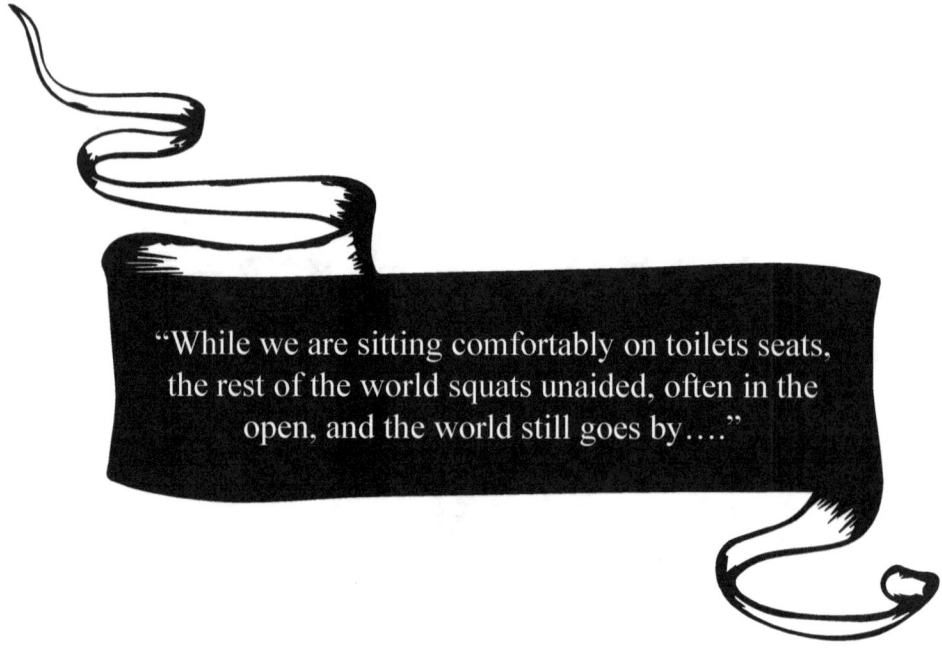

"While we are sitting comfortably on toilets seats, the rest of the world squats unaided, often in the open, and the world still goes by...."

In this Chapter I will explore what a nomad might encounter long-term. This is intended for the full-time nomad who will eventually cease to be a nomad and will settle themselves in a culture or simply staying there for years before moving on. It is a rather different kind of chapter in style. Here I will use many examples and quotations to give a better practical understanding of the expat experience. It is more historical and academic, perhaps. This is due to the fact that the people who were previously engaged in the nomadic lifestyle were hippies on the road, artists, and other undefined groups who were eventually labeled as "expats".

Overseas and Overwhelmed

The word "expatriate" evokes images of the Lost Generation writers and artists in 1920s Paris. This group includes Gertrude Stein, Alice B. Toklas, Henry Miller, Josephine Baker, Ezra Pound, Ernest Hemingway, and many others. They formed an expat community that gathered at the salons and cafes of Paris.

Gertrude Stein wrote *"America is my country, and Paris is my hometown."*

While Stein--like other members of the expat community–regarded Paris as home, she rarely integrated with the French locals. Some never even bothered to learn the language. They left the United States because they no longer connected to its politics and culture. Ironically, in Paris, they lived among other US citizens, rarely connecting with the people of France. This alienated them from their country of birth, while disconnecting from their chosen "hometown."

Sadly, twenty-first century expats engage in the same type of behavior. Some people come to a new country but choose to live in gated communities, isolating themselves from any kind of local contact or communication. If someone fails to understand them, they simply repeat their sentences in their native language, only louder.

Eventually, the expat lifestyle overwhelms them. Feeling frustrated, lonely, and helpless, many return home. Others stay, but use social media communities to post nasty comments about their adopted country. Ironically, bad-mouthing their local country prevents them from getting the help they need. Many locals frequent the expat social media groups, either to practice their second language or to befriend and assist the people who have chosen their country as their new "hometown." So if you come across them, try to mediate or even to persuade them to integrate themselves. They have probably a lot to give to the community they chose as their new home--they simply have not found a way to make that interaction possible. Help them out!

The words "community" and "communication" stem from Latin words, which mean to join, unite, make common, share, and fellowship. Without communication, there is no community.

While I personally never had too much interaction with a closed expat community, I asked Lisa Marie Mercer, a travel writer, to describe her experiences with communication around the world. This approach will clarify the following:

1) the need for language and non-verbal skills , 2) working as part of the local system, and 3) working as a volunteer. The subjects are very broad and what is described here are examples to serve as thought-provoking hints, not essays.

The Case for Cultural Communication

The Mark Twain quote "T*ravel is fatal to prejudice, bigotry and narrow-mindedness,*" embodies one of the basic truisms of travel. We conquer prejudice, bigotry and narrow-mindedness through communication. Inadvertent miscommunication can send the wrong message. Likewise, over-reacting to something that was not meant as an insult can trigger unneeded stress and conflict. For example, in Spanish, the word "negro" simply refers to the color black. It is not meant as an insult.

Language Barriers

Never underestimate the importance of learning the local language, but realize that regional variations might send you back to square one. If you sang "Vamos a la Playa" during your disco years, you will be surprised to discover that it is pronounced with a "sh," instead of an "s." If you study Italian in Rome, then visit the Abruzzi Coast, you might experience similar communication issues because of the different dialects.

Language barriers can affect your ability to:

- Explain your illness or injury to doctor or emergency room staff
- Explain which medications you take in your home country
- Report a crime
- Understand the nuances of the residency process
- Purchase a new home and understand the negotiation process
- Open a bank account
- Start a business
- Feel accepted within your new community
- Ask for directions
- Maintain your dignity
- Order food to your liking

Communicating in Italy

While traveling by train from Rome to Perugia, Lisa sat near a couple from the United States. As the train approached the station, they saw a sign that read "Gabinetti." The man turned to his wife and said "We're coming into Gabinetti." When they saw that the approach to each station has a "Gabinetti" sign, they realized that they were confused. "Gabinetti" means bathrooms! A kindly Italian gentleman used gestures – for which the Italians are famous – to explain the situation.

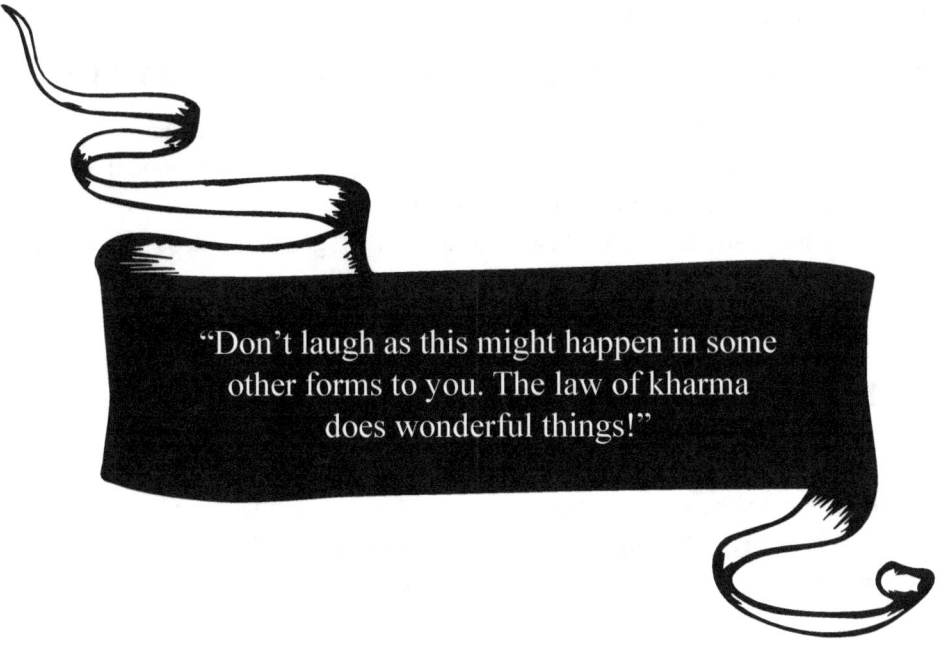

"Don't laugh as this might happen in some other forms to you. The law of kharma does wonderful things!"

On a more serious note, Lisa's summer in Perugia took place during the year of the Iranian hostage crisis. She had no idea that Perugia had a medical school, which had a large population of Iranian students. The Italian language classroom consisted of students from all corners of the globe. Daniela, the instructor, sensed the hostility between the US and Iranian students. Her solution: she had the students talk it out amongst themselves–in Italian–with students from other countries joining in on the debate. At the end of the summer, they all got along.

Communication is not just about words. Body language and gesture play a key role. I discovered this on my solo trip to Egypt in 1981–the summer after the Sadat assassination. I planned to visit Cairo, Luxor, and Aswan, but was dismayed to discover that my travel agent had messed up my reservations. Two local tour guides offered assistance. One stayed with me. The other discussed the issue with the ticket agent. He occasionally gestured to me and the other tour guide, letting them know the progress of the situation.

Reading the gesture and body language, I was sure that all was lost and that nothing could be done. I was wrong. The gestures actually meant that all was well. The next day, I took my flight to Luxor. Even better, I had no problems for the rest of the trip.

In Middle and Far Eastern countries, learning the written and spoken language is easier said than done. Until you find some form of communication, you will need to interpret the non-verbal messages, and avoid inadvertent insults with your own body language and gesture.

Learning and Interpreting Local Gesture and Body Language

As we mentioned in chapter one, gesture and body language are just as important as your verbal language skills. Start by befriending a bilingual local and ask about the meanings of different types of gestures.

YouTube also has an extensive collection of gesture videos for different languages.

A Skyscanner video shows
16 Rude and Interesting Gestures From Around the World https://www.youtube.com/watch?v=a1b6MGoxekY

Pimsleur Approach, the language school, features a video titled
American Hand Gestures in Different Cultures: 7 Ways to Get Yourself in Trouble Abroad https://www.youtube.com/watch?v=fRQSRed58XM

Anthropologist Desmond Morris has a brilliant video on cultural gestures
www.youtube.com/watch?v=fRQSRed58XM

For a more targeted approach, search YouTube for gesture and body language in your specific country of residence

Sensitive Topics

Intelligent, well-educated people often have strong views on specific topics. When living overseas, expressing your ideas is not always a good thing. For example, the news media has a current infatuation with Uruguay's President Jose Mujica, "The World's Poorest President." Many Uruguayans feel the same way. Others do not. In contrast, the press is not too fond of Argentina's Cristina Fernandez, but many Argentinians will defend her with the same fervor that they once reserved for Evita Peron. And then there's President Obama... Parallels exist in other corners of the globe. Test the waters before you pontificate your beliefs to a local. Some cultures enjoy political discourse. Others, Asian countries especially, consider it rude.

Here is just a short list sensitive subjects in different countries and cultures:
- Soccer in South America
- Baseball, especially in Boston, Massachusetts, USA
- Prominent political figures
- Hitler in Germany

If you're from the USA, don't call yourself "American." South and Central Americans are also American.

The Corporate Expat

In her novel titled *The Joy Luck Club*, author Amy Tan writes, "Is the largest problem here that they are literally speaking different languages or that they just don't understand each other, maybe because of cultural barriers?" Tan uses her experiences as a Chinese-American to express the loneliness, isolation, and other emotions shared by people who feel like outsiders.

US citizens who join the corporate culture in China might experience similar issues, but on a larger scale. Hanna Lee of the University of Nevada wrote a dissertation titled <u>International Communication Adjustments.</u> Her paper examines the cultural issues experienced by expatriate managers of China's growing list of hotel venues. She writes:

"China has been notoriously known for its reluctance to adopt foreign values, and for its insistence on its own set of strong nationalistic ideals. And when expatriate managers return from their oversea assignments, they often blame culture shock as well as the stress from various cultural confrontations for their low satisfaction from the works done abroad."

Lee notes that the primary disparities between Eastern and Western culture lie in the difference between individualism and collectivism. Chinese collectivism has roots in the Confucian philosophy, whose basic tenets state that:

- The rights of families, communities, and the overall collective supersede the rights of the individual.
- Workers should do what is best for the society as a whole, rather than what is best for themselves.
- Non-conformity is a serious character defect

Other disconnects exist between Eastern and Western Cultures. The Westerner might view the Chinese commitment to parental obedience as an outdated cultural value. They might perceive humility as lack of confidence, and unquestioned cooperation as an innate fear of conflict and lack of initiative.

China is just one example of how cultural confusion can interfere with the workflow. As such, a number of international hospitality organizations have developed cross-cultural training programs for their expatriate staff. If you plan to, or are currently performing a job in a different country, it is not your place to change their corporate culture. Learn to accept it and work within the system.

The Expat Volunteer

In June of 2014, in Newburyport, MA, Pilates instructor Clare Dunphy accompanied her husband, Dr. Sadru Hemani, on a medical mission to Jordan. The couple arrived within miles of a military border. Their goal: to provide medical care to thousands who escaped from the current military chaos in Syria. This was a complicated mission for the Flying Doctors. The refugees, who arrived exhausted and dehydrated, needed clearance to enter Jordan. Once they reached the medical area, Clare directed them to the appropriate doctor. Although the couple did not speak the local language, English speaking medical students provided translation assistance. Somehow they managed to communicate. Clare even taught Pilates sessions to some of the refugees. At the end of their trip, she posted the following status update on her Facebook page:

"A Syrian refugee came over to say thank -you ... Not just for the medical care but for the way were cared for and respected the people. Talk about living the dream! The Flying Doctors of America rocked this one and I was honored to help."

Taking the Volatility Out of Voluntarism

Given the political volatility of the region, cultural clashes on the Jordan mission could have triggered a disaster. Instead, it was "a wonderful and life-changing experience." Many expatriates romanticize the idea of volunteering for a week, a month, or even a year. Some, however, just aren't prepared. Environmentalist Dave Tracey writes:

"There is both a moral and social responsibility attaching to these experiences of foreign cultures, and if nothing awakens in our own soul, making claims and demands upon us, calling us to change the way we live, then we have been merely parasites and invaders."

Even if you are on a "medical mission," do not act like a missionary. You are not there to change the lifestyles of the people you help. You are not there to convert them. Patronizing and arrogant attitudes will cause epic failure. As Clare Dunphy notes, her time in Jordan was a "life-changing experience."

Their willingness to learn from local cultures is what makes the Flying Doctors a success. Clare and Sadru have been on other medical missions to places such as Honduras, Peru and the Amazon Jungle. During the Madre de Dios Peru mission, the team devoted some time to exploring the medicinal plants of the region. This type of sharing promoted mutual respect.

Volunteers must have a clear understanding of their role as cross-cultural development agents. This goes beyond providing a checklist of cultural attributes and no-no's. A statement on the Palms Australia website sums it up:

"Understanding their own cultural adjustment can help a volunteer realize when their judgments reflect their own process rather than some "truth" about their hosts. Learning strategies to pull through culture shock, build cross-cultural relationships, understand the impact of one's own culture and personality and seek local advice are essential if their work is to be sustainable."

Holistic Communication Skills

Thanks to the World Wide Web, expatriates now have a diverse library of resources for learning new languages and communication skills. Some websites even offer free online language lessons. Many of these are ad-supported, and some will urge you to upgrade to their paid, premium version. Most, however, provide an excellent starting point and offer a way to learn the basic, everyday phrases of the language. Here are some of them:

- **OpenCulture**
  http://www.openculture.com/freelanguagelessons Open Culture lists three-hundred free language-learning websites for forty-eight different languages. As the ultimate open source website in cyberspace, they also link to free films, free classic literature, and art galleries around the world. If you want to learn more about the history, culture, and religious customs of your chosen country, Open Culture will serve you an extensive list of free online courses on almost any topic.
- **Digital Dialects**
  http://www.digitaldialects.com Offering courses for seventy different languages, this free website uses animated games as a learning tool. Perfect for bringing out your inner child
- **Busuu**
  http://www.busuu.com/enc Best described as a social network for

language learning, Busuu offers courses in twelve different languages. The site gives you the opportunity to practice languages with native speakers through the video-chat feature.

o **Duolingo**
https://www.duolingo.com It offers free lessons in English, French, Spanish, German, Italian and Portuguese. The learning process takes the form of short form of quizzes, which require listening, speaking and writing. The site has an app that facilitates competitions between you and your Facebook friends.

o **Destinos**
http://learner.org/series/ Destino provides more than an effective way to learn Spanish. It offers an engrossing story, that will keep you coming back for more. As the story unfolds, Los Angeles-based lawyer Raquel Rodríguez receives a communication from the family of Fernando Castillo. Castillo has just learned that his first wife, Rosario, did not die in the Spanish Civil War. Castillo hires Rodríguez to search for Rosario. The lawyer takes her search through different Spanish speaking areas, including Seville and Madrid, Spain; Buenos Aires, Argentina; San Juan and San Germán, Puerto Rico; and Mexico. As you follow her journey, you learn the dialects of the different countries,

Other Language Learning Options can be found in the appendix.

When possible, forgo any type of transportation and walk from place to place. The Italians, for example, have turned walking into a cultural tradition. During passeggiata, as it's called, people dress up and stroll through the central areas of the village or city. In her books titled The Passeggiata and Popular Culture in an Italian Town, author Giovanna P. Del Negro notes that passeggiata is also *"a socially sanctioned opportunity for flirting and courting."* Parents encourage such behavior, because "the rhetorical skills learned in the piazza become useful in the marriage market, the work place and the complex politics of the town."

I leave you with this thought:

"Foreign lands never yield their secrets to a traveler. The best they offer are tantalizing snippets, just enough to inflame the imagination. The secrets they do reveal are your own - the ones you have kept from yourself. And this is reason enough to travel, to leave home."

Graeme Sparks

Chapter 9

Is Time To Leave You Play

What you have read so far is meant to provide you with a rough idea how to turn your life around if you ever thought you could go traveling for a living. It is however just one way; if it differs from what you might end up using, don't shoot the messenger!

It is impossible to make a bulletproof method of adopting a lifestyle that epitomizes freedom. Your success will come from growing into a wise, unconventional person by weaving a tapestry from enriching experiences and a multitude of life lessons. This book is just a tiny piece of the entire puzzle; you'll have to figure out how it fits in.

Read it again if you need to clarify or reinforce anything. Keep it in your nomad toolbox along with the exercises you used to build your Dreamboard, overcome fears, and find your passion. Complementary aids such as a workbook are also available at **www.goingnomadbook.com** in case you need extra help.

I wish that my personal stories have succeeded in igniting a desire, and maybe had you laughing. You soon will add your own funny stories as well as your deep and meaningful ones. I shared mine in a book with you—please, if you feel like sharing them with me too, I would love to hear them. Otherwise, don't keep them private--share them with your friends, colleagues, and relatives. Sharing travel tales makes life more enjoyable..

I hope the Magician provided you with opportunities for reflection, but the ultimate truth is yours, the last word always your own. You are the driver of your life, so if you choose to not to engage in the rat race any longer, you will have stepped out of a system that has indoctrinated you since childhood, made you follow rules blindly, pushed you toward familiar "tried and tested" strategies. Although you may have questioned it and found it unsatisfying, it did provide you with achievements and rewards. It felt safe. So I hope your journey can find in the nomadic freedom as a more fulfilling answer to your quest.

You might not define yourself as a nomad or traveler, as you are always in a perennial transition, living your life in one place yet putting your heart in your numerous epic travels. Don't be concerned: remember that you will not be defined by a label, but by yourself.

When you count your blessings, I hope traveling will be one of them. Never for one minute forget how fortunate you are. For millions of people, being alive and making it to tomorrow is the only reality. They might be nomads out of necessity for survival, but they will never have the freedom to *choose* travel . You might meet them, they might be catalysts of your flow, or their generosity might be a humbling lesson. You owe it to them to take the opportunity to reach out, whenever you can. Don't go numb, letting them pass you by. You probably need them more than they need you!

It is their land, their culture, their heritage; you are a temporary visitor who eventually moves on. In that short time, you can choose to leave your footprint, you can choose to be useful. Accept that you'll never be a native, but make sure that you are never a burden.

Rejecting the culture you were born into will not qualify you! "The Dropout" is not a mindset I chose to explore in this book because it is not needed anymore. A nomad must find a proactive, useful way to engage in life so that a rippling effect can be seen in the world at large.

Your traveling might teach you that is possible to dream of a better world where hunger and poverty have no place, where there is enough food and water to go around, where the animals and trees are not in danger of extinction, where the quest for sustainable energy sources can be achieved by letting go of greed. You share this dream with the people who live in total poverty as well as with the other nomads you meet on the road, so that you can dream bigger ones.

The indigenous elders are waiting for us to wake up, as we have forgotten how to dream, and to take charge by becoming epic warriors.

Rainbow Tribe

The sun rose on a magical new day...
Over the whole earth they came,
The people of every colour,
Sister, Brother, Father, Mother
Traveling over many a land
People of the Rainbow
Children of the Way,
with a fresh glow
Finding their way
Star within...
More and more joined,
a song for the soul...
A new way to live,
A new way to see,
It happened this way...
And a new song,
It came from within
If you can find the Star,
Within then you will find...
What is... What was...
And what will be... you see,
It happened this way...
from within,
The people of the Way
The Rainbow Tribe...

- Author Unknown

Magician final words:

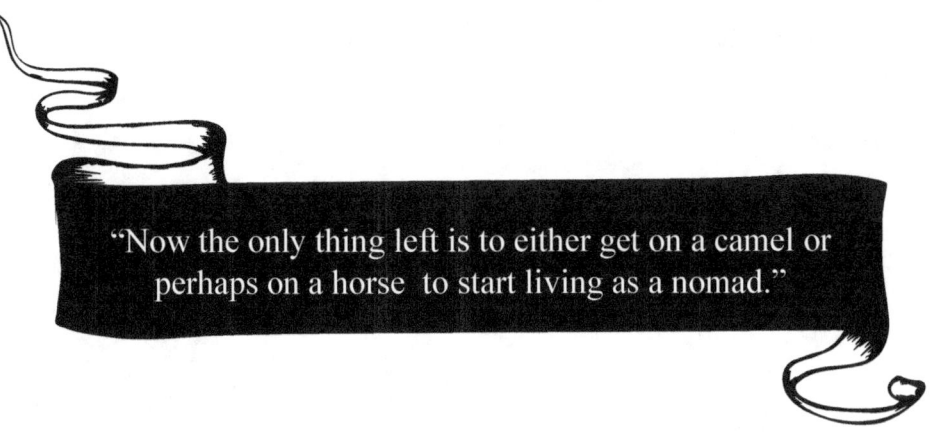

"Now the only thing left is to either get on a camel or perhaps on a horse to start living as a nomad."

To be continued by you!
Go fill your life with wonder!

APPENDIX:

CHAPTER 1: Reasons For Travel

- **Education**—Forget what you have previously learned or re-evaluate what you took for granted; the Nomadic Traveling School awaits you to deliver its wonders!
- **Chill Out**—Travel slows you down so that you can take on one issue at the time. Work out your stresses and take things slow.
- **Searching for Happiness**—While you can only find that inside you, traveling will make you more cheerful and you will feel as light as a feather!
- **Transition**—New career? Break up? Or simply time to reflect? Traveling can point you towards a stream of opportunities. Readjust your compass and breathe in fresh life!
- **New Skills**—Is there something you have always wanted to learn? To improve on? You might also stumble upon something you didn't know you wanted to learn. Broaden your horizons.
- **Finding Yourself**—Not many will admit this, but this might be the number one reason, even when not apparent at first. The twenty-first century offers the perfect opportunity for everyone to embrace the ultimate search to become a nomad and prosper.
- **It Feels Good for the Soul**—You are going to feel renewed and invigorated!
- **New Perspective**—Travel will change or challenge your worldview; reality is not what you see in the media.
- **New Confidence**—Life is full of obstacles. Overcoming them while traveling has a different flavor and turns you into a wise, action-driven person. Prove to yourself that YOU can!
- **Having a Story**—Your life can be a book full of experiences that you might like to share with the world
- **Doing Something New**—Eating new food, learning a new language, learning new sport, having new adventures, and developing new habits.
- **It is my Dream!** —You are the dream-maker, so what about the dream-doer? Dreams do come true!
- **Time to Heal**—There is a time in life when this can be your reason. If you feel this, then don't wait any longer: your calling is real. Whatever you do, don't ignore it.
- **Renewal and Enthusiasm**—If you feel low, drained, de-motivated or worse, that life is no longer exciting, passionate, or worth the energy, traveling is your medicine.

- **Love**—You will meet plenty of people, who will put you in a position to create long-lasting relationships, even if your location, culture, and lifestyle do not match.

EXERCISE:
Overcoming fears (to be done with a partner).

In this exercise, I draw upon a very famous technique used by NIP, a science that helps modify human behavior.

Fears that keep us from achieving what we want are often irrational; it is time to deal with them once and for all. However, use this exercise with common sense: some fears are healthy indicators of objectively dangerous situations. I leave it to you to assess if that is the case.

For this exercise, choose one fear that stops you from achieving your traveling goal. If you have many, just pick one. i.e. fear of flying (Let your partner prompting you from now on)

P: "Okay, how bad does it feel? Please get a picture in your head. Notice how that feels." (Pause). "Where do you see it?" *(If there is no response prompt: "Top, right? Is it big or small? Black and white, or in color?")*

P: "Now, what did you have for breakfast? I know, this question seems irrelevant, but just answer it...Great!"

VISUALIZATION: (done with eyes closed):

P: "Now, close your eyes. Imagine yourself sitting in a cinema in the front row. The screen in front of you is blank. Can you see yourself? Good."

(If no response, keep asking until they can see the scene.)

P: "I would like you to imagine that you can leave your body and float into the projection room. See yourself sitting in the front row of the theatre. Can you see it?"*(Keep asking until they can see the scene.)*

P: "Next, float back so that you are again in the front row. This time, you are watching the screen which has yourself in it, like a movie, showing this fear stopping you from traveling. Just imagine the scenario with moving pictures on the screen, just as if you are watching a movie. Great! Enjoy the story until it ends. Let me know when it does..." (Pause) if they don't say anything ask "Has it finished?" once they say yes say "Great, Now watch it again, but this time in black and white."*(if it takes a long time, ask them to fast-forward to the end. Once that minute is past, ask them to blackout the screen.)*

P: "Good! Now start the movie again, this time run it backwards from the end. When you get to the beginning, black out the screen."

(Repeat the steps: play the movie in color, then repeat in black and white,

then backwards in color. Keep asking how they feel; eventually, after perhaps three times through, they will have no emotion, the experience of watching the movie will be totally neutral.)

P: "Great! Now, open your eyes. Is it raining outside? I know, another irrelevant question! Just answer it."

P: "Now, close your eyes again, and think about travel, happy memories or images of travel. Let them surface."

(Wait until they are ready.)

P: "Now, see yourself in the theater again, and begin to run the old movie --the one you did before. But this time, in the left corner, there is a small window with the happy travel memories or images in it. Both movies play simultaneously; now you see the big screen, now you see the left corner, and so on."

(Wait until they are clear.)

P: (After a minute has passed) "Now, switch the screens: the happy image is on the whole of the screen and the old negative one is in the corner."

(Ask them to repeat this in their mind five times.)

P: "Now, watch the happy movie again. Does it feel better? Do you feel more confident? Do you enjoy it more?"

END WITH EYES OPEN

If you don't have much success with this exercise, do it again on another day. The first time might seem odd, the second time it will be more familiar, easier and more effective. The old fear will either disappear entirely or have less of an impact and you will feel more in control.

CHAPTER 2

Here are some directories for e-tutors:

For language teachers:

http://www.verbalplanet.com

http://www.homeeddirectory.com

Or use Alexa (a website measuring web traffic) to find the most popular and reputable online schools:

http://www.alexa.com/topsites/category/Reference/Education/K_through_12/Home_Schooling/Middle_and_High_School

CHAPTER 4: The passion finder

EXERCISE:

Take a Journal, switch off your mobile phone and make sure you will be undisturbed for the next 45 minutes. If it helps, play a piece of music to get you to relax. Choose one that evokes happy memories or even a time where you felt on top of the world, inspired and authentic.

Do you have a memory of such a time? (Take few minutes to let a memory surface)

If you don't have such a memory, just imagine being happy. What facial expression would you have? Assume that position, as physiology can trigger the emotion more easily.

Once you are satisfied and you definitely feel in a positive mood, take out your journal, as you will spend some time answering a few questions:
- What did you enjoy doing as a child?
- What activities do you most enjoy doing at work? (Consider previous jobs too)
- What activities are most afraid of doing? Circle the ones you would like to conquer and achieve.

- List a few things that are great about you and your achievements. Consider also asking: what do other people say you would be really good at?
- What life achievements would you want to pass on as a legacy or be remembered for, things to celebrate?
- What would you love to do if time/money/commitments/self-esteem were no issue?
- What do you love to do as a hobby?
- What are some things you desire, yet hear yourself saying, "No, I can't do it?."

Now, considering all the previous answers, make a list of all the skills you have, and all the skills you would love to have. Spend as long as you like considering your lists. Don't worry if your mind has gone blank; this is only a defense mechanism to keep you from deep-seated emotions guarded by a protective ego.

Once you feel clearer in your head, perhaps even excited, ask yourself this final question with your eyes closed: If your life were a dream, how would you imagine it to be? Let yourself come up with images as if you were watching a movie, relax into it, enjoy it. Do this for five minutes or so.

After you have answered all questions, see if you can find three things that stand out as a thread in your life. It can be something you enjoy and get lost in, or something you find almost effortless. The best would be to find something that frightens you. This is because when you feel a strong passion, if you hear yourself saying, "I can't do this," or "I don't deserve this," this can be an indication of problems with self-esteem or self-worth. These are roadblocks you have to overcome, otherwise you'll never flourish and be happy. The exercise has shown your passions, living them is not easy, yet is rewarding once you learn. This quote (used in a speech by Nelson Mandela) sum it up.

"Our deepest fear is not that we are inadequate. Our deepest fear is that we are powerful beyond measure. It is our light, not our darkness, that most frightens us. We ask ourselves, who am I to be brilliant, gorgeous, talented, fabulous? Actually, who are you not to be? You are a child of God. Your playing small doesn't serve the world. There's nothing enlightened about shrinking so that other people won't feel insecure around you. We are all meant to shine, as children do. We were born to make manifest the glory of God that is within us. It's not just in some of us; it's in everyone. And as we let our own light shine, we unconsciously give other people permission to do the same. As we're liberated from our own fear, our presence automatically liberates others."

From: **A Return to Love: Reflections on the Principles of A Course in Miracles**
- Author Marianne Williamson

CHAPTER 4: Learning a foreign Language
Other Language Learning Options

- Organize a weekly language exchange group between locals and expats. Take it one step further, by sharing recipes and culture-specific crafts. This will teach you how to learn the names of different foods, cooking utensils and craft supplies.
- Participate in local activities, and don't spend all your time with the expat groups.
- Watch local television shows to learn the common colloquialisms. In Spanish speaking countries, the gestures and facial expressions are so dramatic that you don't need to know the language to understand what they are saying. Crackle.com shows foreign TV and US shows and movies. Less restrictive than Hulu, you can watch the channel in twenty-two countries. Show are available in three languages: English, Spanish and Portuguese. Choose which language your prefer for the spoken language, and which language you want for the sub-titles.
- Show a willingness to learn the local language. Patronize smaller, family run stores, and learn the local translation for "how do you say this in (local language)." Point to the item in question write down the translation. Most people really love to help, especially if you shop at their store on a regular basis. Instead of buying imported brands from your country of origin, experiment with local brands.
- Load your smart phone with commonly used phrases in the local language. If you have an important appointment, type in these phrases and rehearse them before you leave the house. When you get to your meeting, preface your communication with the local translations for "I'm sorry, I do not speak your language very well." The person might know your language. If they don't, they will speak a bit more slowly.
- Use public modes of transportation. Although car transport might offer convenience, it isolates you from other people. Trains, buses, and ferries provide perfect opportunities for meeting and communicating.

PHOTO CREDITS:

INTRODUCTION:
1) cc attribution license by flowcomm
https://www.flickr.com/photos/flowcomm/8273485765

CHAPTER 1
2) cc attribution license by Nanette Saylor
https://www.flickr.com/photos/wisewellwoman/5227629874

CHAPTER 2
1) cc attribution license by Dojorus
https://www.flickr.com/photos/54706868@N06
2) cc attribution license by charlie marshall
https://www.flickr.com/photos/100915417@N07/
3) cc attribution license by David W.
https://www.flickr.com/photos/davidw
4) cc attribution license by Miran
https://www.flickr.com/photos/miran/

CHAPTER 3
1) cc attribution license by Miran
https://www.flickr.com/photos/miran/
2) cc attribution license by Keoni Cabral
https://www.flickr.com/photos/keoni101
3) cc attribution license by J. Morrow
https://www.flickr.com/photos/donotlick
4) cc attribution license by Sarah Nicols
https://www.flickr.com/photos/pocheco/

CHAPTER 4
1) Scc attribution license bySteven Zwerink
https://www.flickr.com/photos/stevenzwerink/6649030521
2) cc attribution license by Dimitry Terekhow
https://www.flickr.com/photos/44400809@N07

CHAPTER 5
1) creative common license thanks to Leland
https://www.flickr.com/photos/lel4nd

CHAPTER 6
1) cc attribution license by Leiland Francisco
https://www.flickr.com/photos/lel4nd
2) cc attribution license by Keoni Cabral
https://www.flickr.com/photos/keoni101

CHAPTER 7
1) cc attribution license by Giuseppe Milo
https://www.flickr.com/photos/giuseppemilo

CHAPTER 9
1) cc attribution license by camels
https://www.flickr.com/photos/wonderlane/5208126799

RESOURCES

Carefully hand-picked links. Instead of listing comparison sites, travel search engines, budget airlines, travel gear acquisition, and apartment rentals, this list focuses on resources to help you shift perspective, connect with other travelers, inspire and dream!

www.tropicalmba.com Blog and podcast, dedicated to the growing movement of location-independent entrepreneurs worldwide.

www.teleport.org Offers softwares for the mobile lifestyle. Currently, they have apps that help with budgeting and cost of living figures for different world-wide locations. Helps with finding a suitable itinerary.

www.360training.com One of the best site to learn new skills.

www.seasonalemployment.com Directory to find seasonal positions.

www.flexjobs.com Directory for telecommuting, location-independent jobs.

www.fotolia.com One of many sites you can use to sell your photos, YouTube has tutorials on what to photograph and how to be profitable in selling your photos online.

http://www.independenttraveler.com/travel-tips/packing-and- accessories/the-ultimate-guide-to-travel-packing
Here you will find the best tips on packing light and stay light.

http://typicalprogrammer.com/how-i-work-as-a-digital-nomad
If you are a programmer, or are keen to learn a coding language, you will find this inspirational story captivating.

https://www.worldnomads.com/travel-insurance
One of the best travel insurances.

http://www.flyertalk.com This has a very informative travel forum on many subject. It is also popular in the travel-hacking community.

http://polyglotclub.com If you speak many languages or are willing to in a near future, you are welcome to join like-minded people.

http://polyglotberlin.com This is a very cool conference. It touches on many travel-related subjects, and is not exclusive to polyglots!

http://wwoofinternational.org Best way to learn organic farming.

https://www.worldwidebrands.com If you want to sell physical products without inventory or having the hassle of shipping it, you need a dropshipper wholesale or manufacturing company. This is a paid service to get a reliable directory. WARNING: You should first learn the pros and cons of starting such a business. Popular for an Ebay- or Amazon-type platform.

http://appcrawlr.com/android-apps/best-apps-sms-translation SMS translator app for your smartphones.

http://techpp.com/2013/06/05/best-translating-apps On the same note as above, but includes iPhone apps.

http://www.travelpod.com Here is a platform you can use for your travel blog. It is basic but takes away the learning curve of using Wordpress.

http://flightfox.com Crowd-sourced travel expert helping you to find best deals on flights.

http://www.expeditionengineering.com Expedition Engineering specializes in creating custom adventures to remote locations all over the world. They challenge and encourage clients to dream big.

www.ingramcontent.com/pod-product-compliance
Lightning Source LLC
Chambersburg PA
CBHW070624300426
44113CB00010B/1642